TROPHIES OF HIS GRACE

Copyright © 2020 by Deborah Rae Stricklin

Published by Dream Releaser Enterprises

All rights reserved. Under International Copyright Law, no part of this publication may be reproduced, stored, or transmitted by any means—electronic, mechanical, photographic (photocopy), recording, or otherwise—without written permission from the publisher.

Unless otherwise indicated all Scripture quotations are taken from the Holy Bible, New Living Translation, copyright ©1996, 2004, 2015 by Tyndale House Foundation. Used by permission of Tyndale House Publishers, Inc., Carol Stream, Illinois 60188. All rights reserved.

Scriptures marked ESV are taken from The Holy Bible, English Standard Version® (ESV®) Copyright © 2001 by Crossway, a publishing ministry of Good News Publishers. All rights reserved.

Scripture quotations marked (NKJV) are taken from the New King James Version®. Copyright © 1982 by Thomas Nelson. Used by permission. All rights reserved.

Cover design by: Joe DeLeon

ISBN: 978-1-950718-71-9 1 2 3 4 5 6 7 8 9 10

Printed in the United States of America

TROPHIES OF HIS GRACE

Capture the Goodness and Glory of the Grace of God

DEBORAH RAE STRICKLIN

Contents

Foreword vii

Introduction ix

Chapter 1. Victorious Grace 11

Chapter 2. Delivered from Pride 19

Chapter 3. From Death to Life 29

Chapter 4. A Matter of Trust 39

Chapter 5. More Than Enough 49

Chapter 6. Perfectly Sane 61

Chapter 7. Moved with Compassion 73

Chapter 8. Rescued and Set Free 81

Chapter 9. Life Happens 91

Chapter 10. Prepare the Way 99

Chapter 11. Grace to Let Go 107

Epilogue 113

Foreword

There is probably no greater need among God's people than to gain a deeper and more enduring understanding of His grace. That has always been true among the people of God, and it is still true today.

That's why I'm glad you're reading this book. Deborah Stricklin understands the grace of God, both from learning biblical truth and also from personally experiencing that truth. In this book, she demonstrates that grace isn't just an idea to know; it is what we need to direct and sustain us through all the peaks and valleys of real life.

As Deborah walks you through key passages from both the Old and New Testaments, be ready to receive one of God's best blessings—a greater understanding and experience of His grace.

Deborah has received God's grace into her own life. And in *Trophies of His Grace*, she has captured the goodness and glory of the grace of God working in the lives of others—ordinary people—and transforming them into His own trophies. God's *trophy case* has room for you, too.

David Guzik
Author, *Enduring Word Bible Commentary*
Teaching Pastor, Calvary Chapel

INTRODUCTION

From my earliest memories, I have always loved God's Word. As a child, I remember reading my red, hardback Bible with great curiosity and genuine desire. To this day, reading the Bible opens my eyes to the beauty of God's character.

When we don't read the Bible, our view of God is limited to the opinions of those who influence us most. So I take every opportunity I am given to encourage God's people to spend time reading His Word.

So many people—including Christians—see God as a punishing taskmaster or disinterested deity. But that is not the God I know. God has always been my greatest love and closest friend.

My God is the faithful Friend, the loving Father, and the merciful Savior portrayed in His Word. And my desire, through this book, is to paint that picture of Him with my words—a picture of the God of grace I've come to know.

The people of the Bible were like you and me. We experience a life with both temptations and victory, and so did they. But God's beautiful grace, which is readily available to those who put their trust in Him, is the thread woven through every story.

As you read about God's gift of grace in the lives of the apostle Paul, King Nebuchadnezzar, Lazarus, Jairus' daughter, Job, the demon-possessed man, and many others, I pray that you will fall in love with the Word of God all over again (or perhaps for the first time) and let God's grace transform your life.

Then you and I, like the biblical heroes of old, can stand together as trophies of God's incredible grace.

—Deborah

CHAPTER 1

Victorious Grace

CHILDHOOD MEMORIES OFTEN draw our minds and emotions back to a time of fewer responsibilities and big imaginations. My childhood memories are reminiscent of carefree days and a simplistic view of life.

I grew up in southern California, where my days were filled with sunshine, the joy of family, and playing outside. During my growing up years, *home* was split between the southern California cities of San Diego and Santa Barbara. My father worked in both cities, so our whole family moved back and forth between them to accommodate his work responsibilities.

Two of my high school years were spent in Santa Barbara, where I reacquainted myself with old friends and made new ones. One new friend who stands out in my mind was Andrea. My friend Andrea lived about ten houses away from mine, on a street that I'll call *the horseshoe.*

Our street was u-shaped, which made coming in and going out of our little group of houses rather straightforward. People living on our street entered at one end of the horseshoe or the other. If residents got in the habit of always traveling the same half of the horseshoe—going back the same way they came—they might never drive past the houses on the opposite side of the street.

We lived on the corner of what I rather shortsightedly assumed was the primary entrance to the horseshoe. But my friend Andrea lived right in the middle—at the top (or bottom, as it were)—of the horseshoe. She was known not only to my side, but also to those who seemed like strangers on the other side.

Andrea was the majorette for Santa Barbara's San Marcos High School, where I attended. She was a sort of celebrity—a baton-twirling wonder—in our small neighborhood. But spinning batons (plural!) wasn't her only talent. Spinning knives, fire batons, and rifles were also part of her repertoire. And the little portion of the street that made up the curve of the horseshoe was Andrea's chosen practice space.

With the open sky above and plenty of room in the street, she was able to throw her twirling objects high into the air and march out all her dance steps in between. No one living on our u-shaped street wanted to interrupt her practices. So when Andrea was outside practicing, those who lived on the opposite side of the horseshoe from us exited on their side, and we exited on ours.

I had many opportunities to watch Andrea practice, and I was mesmerized every time. Not wanting to disturb her concentration, I sat quietly on the curb—just far enough away that she wouldn't notice me. Her ability to throw her batons with such accuracy and catch them with perfect timing simply amazed me. And when she twirled fire batons without injury, I could hardly contain my astonishment.

Friday nights during football season were exciting as everyone gathered to watch the games. But the halftime shows were worthy of as much attention as the entire game. Our drill team, cheerleaders, band, and Andrea—our amazing majorette—marched onto the field and wowed the crowds during every home game.

As it turned out, though, Andrea wasn't just our halftime wonder. While many of us teenagers were helping with yard work and playing local sports during our weekends, Andrea was competing in statewide and nationwide twirling competitions.

Andrea's bedroom walls, lined with trophies, gave witness to her numerous victories in those competitions. I remember the first time I walked into Andrea's room and saw the many trophies she had earned. I was absolutely overwhelmed by the number of trophies on the shelves. There were small trophies, large trophies, trophies with batons, trophies shaped like chalices, and trophies of many other varieties. But they all had one thing in common; they all commemorated the victories achieved by Andrea her amazing talent, her persistent practice, and her unyielding desire to win.

☙ ❧

Throughout history, victories have often been commemorated with trophies. But these haven't always been the kind of trophies we think of today. The concept of trophies as remembrances of victories and conquests has existed for perhaps as long as mankind has been fighting wars. The word "trophy" comes from the Latin word *trophaeum*, which is "an ancient Greek or Roman monument commemorating a military victory."[1]

In ancient Greece, victorious soldiers gathered the spoils of war from their defeated foes and displayed them on a fixed object, such as a tree. This was a way of proving the supremacy of the victors. They were, in effect, trophies. Over time, trophies also became symbols of victory in sports competitions and academic contests, as well as symbols of achievement for actors, writers, artists, scientists, and others.

Today's trophies are made of a variety of materials, the most elite being made of precious metals, expensive crystal, and gems. As I contemplated the use of trophies, I began imagining another kind that is quite different. This kind of trophy is more precious than gold and more powerfully symbolic of triumph than those commemorating anyone's personal achievements.

I'm talking about the trophies of human lives transformed by the grace of our victorious God.

---

1 "Trophaeum." Merriam-Webster.com Dictionary, Merriam-Webster, https://www.merriam-webster.com/dictionary/trophaeum.

As I read the Word of God, I'm awestruck by the changed lives I read about—lives touched by God's matchless grace. When I read the stories of people such as Nebuchadnezzar, Lazarus, Jairus' daughter, Peter, Paul, the unnamed man in the graveyard,[2] and the widow of Nain, I am overwhelmed with gratitude as I consider how God's grace transforms people.

And the Lord is still doing that today! If we're at all paying attention, we can see God's grace at work in the lives of people all around us.

Last night, I served in the Bridge Ministry[3] here in my hometown of Nashville—as I do most Tuesday nights. The ministry is led by a wonderful lady named Candy Christmas. The Bridge Ministry meets weekly under the Jefferson Street Bridge to feed and provide clothing to the poor and homeless. The life-giving message of Jesus Christ is preached there each week. It has been my privilege to participate in this ministry for over four years now.

Each week, people are given the opportunity to receive Christ and grow through the preaching of the Word, and many of those who attend wisely take advantage of that opportunity. As a result, many of the Bridge Ministry participants experience blessings over time as they obediently follow Christ and His Word. It is not unusual to hear testimonies in those evening services about our guests obtaining jobs, finding apartments, or in other ways bettering their lives.

During the service last night, Candy asked a man named Michael—one of our guests—to stand. She shared how he had been homeless, destitute, and living in drunken solitude just three short years ago. He gave his life to Christ and started making wiser decisions with the Holy Spirit's help. Today, he works in a stable job, lives in his own home, and enjoys freedom from addiction.

As Michael stood there last night, before the gathering of over three hundred people, he began to sing the song *Amazing Grace*. My heart was touched as I thought about what God's grace had accomplished in Michael's life. God truly set Michael free from his past ways of living,

---

2 Mark 5:1-20.

3 To find out more about the Bridge Ministry, visit https://www.bridgeministry.org/the-bridge.html

and he is growing in obedience to God's Word. He is experiencing the blessings that accompany God's grace at work in his life.

☙ ❧

As I contemplate God's amazing grace, I think of the freedom we experience through new life in Christ, the power we walk in through the Holy Spirit's influence in our lives, and the wisdom we enjoy in knowing and obeying God's Word.

Grace incorporates all of these things, and many more. From beginning to end, the process of the Christian life is dependent on God's grace. Through His grace, the Lord draws us, saves us, fills us, transforms us, and leads us home.

First, grace is given as a gift to unbelievers so they are able to hear and respond to the gospel message and experience salvation.

> *God saved you by his grace when you believed. And you can't take credit for this; it is a gift from God.*
> (Ephesians 2:8)

> *For the grace of God has been revealed, bringing salvation to all people.* (Titus 2:11)

Then, God's grace is given to us as believers to work in us and enable us in Christian growth. Having experienced grace, we are encouraged to learn obedience, partake of God's power, and bear witness to the transformation in us, made possible only by God's actions. Our ongoing and progressive intimacy with Christ is made possible by His gift of grace working in and filling our lives.

> *For God is working in you, giving you the desire and the power to do what pleases him.* (Philippians 2:13)

> *You already know these things, dear friends. So be on guard; then you will not be carried away by the errors*

> *of these wicked people and lose your own secure footing. Rather, you must grow in the grace and knowledge of our Lord and Savior Jesus Christ. All glory to him, both now and forever! Amen.* (2 Peter 3:17-18)

> *This High Priest of ours understands our weaknesses, for he faced all of the same testings we do, yet he did not sin. So let us come boldly to the throne of our gracious God. There we will receive his mercy, and we will find grace to help us when we need it most.* (Hebrews 4:15-16)

Finally, believers experience God's amazing grace even in death as He leads us home and shares with us the bounty of heaven.

> *Father, I want these whom you have given me to be with me where I am. Then they can see all the glory you gave me because you loved me even before the world began!* (John 17:24)

In light of its many facets—how grace works in us, through us, and for us—how might we define it? In his letter to the Christians in Rome, the apostle Paul described grace as God's free and undeserved kindness toward us.[4]

Noah Webster, renowned American lexicographer, defined grace as the "favor of God, the spring and source of all the benefits men receive from him." Webster further defined grace as the "favorable influence of God; divine influence or the influence of the spirit, in renewing the heart and restraining from sin."[5]

William Mounce's *Complete Expository Dictionary of Old & New Testament Words* describes grace with these words:

---

4 "It is the same today, for a few of the people of Israel have remained faithful because of God's grace—his undeserved kindness in choosing them. And since it is through God's kindness, then it is not by their good works. For in that case, God's grace would not be what it really is—free and undeserved" (Romans 11:5-6).

5 *American Dictionary of the English Language*, Noah Webster, 1828.

> *Grace is a new domain in which and by which Christians live (Rom. 15:15; 16:20). In this realm sin no longer rules (6:14). By his grace, God affects Christians' personal lives, giving them the ability to obey the gospel from the heart (Rom. 6:17), the ability to work hard (1 Cor. 15:10), and an increase of joy in severe trials (2 Cor. 8:1-2).*[6]

When we consider the richness and the fullness of God's grace, our joy and gratitude for His kindness toward us should overflow. God found us in the depth of our sin—our hearts far from Him—and He rescued us. God's grace extends to us the undeserved kindness of abundant life in Him, which would be completely inaccessible to us except through His benevolence and the sacrifice of His Son, Jesus Christ.

> *All of this is for your benefit. And as God's grace reaches more and more people, there will be great thanksgiving, and God will receive more and more glory.*
>
> (2 Corinthians 4:15)

How kind God is to us!

Although earnest and heartfelt, my attempt to describe the grace I have personally come to know seems, to me, wholly inadequate. But through His Word, God has given us the beautiful evidence of His matchless grace through the visible and obvious transformation of many lives.

> In the [Old Testament], God revealed himself as a God of grace and mercy who showed love to his people, not because they deserved it, but because of his own desire to have a personal relationship with them and to be faithful to the promises he made to Abraham, Isaac and Jacob . . . The [New Testament] focuses on

6 *Complete Expository Dictionary of Old & New Testament Words*, William Mounce, Zondervan, 2006, p. 304.

> the theme of God's grace in the giving of his Son, Jesus, who willingly gave his life for undeserving sinners.[7]

As Christians today, we continue to experience and grow in His grace through His Word and the presence of the Holy Spirit in our lives.

଺ ଻

The lives of those we view as heroes of faith are God's trophies.

The lives of biblical characters, the lives of the followers of Christ throughout the ages, and the lives of people who live among us—whose lives speak to the power of grace today—are all God's trophies.

And yes, your life also is a trophy of God's grace, if you have allowed yourself to be transformed by the Holy Spirit as He works in your life to reveal God's grace to you, in you, and through you.

Throughout the pages of this book, we will search out beautiful, biblical evidence of God's grace revealed in the lives of others and apply what we've encountered to our own lives. Just as my friend Andrea's trophies stand witness to the victories she achieved in competition, transformed lives stand witness to and commemorate the nature and work of God's victorious grace.

7 "Faith and Grace", *Fire Bible: ESV*, Hendrickson Publishers, 2014, pp. 1894-1895.

CHAPTER 2

Delivered from Pride

THE RECOGNITION GIVEN to victors of all kinds is usually well-deserved, and we should celebrate one another's achievements. But when we are the recipients of the recognition, we need to keep in mind that there is an inherent danger in becoming enamored with the applause of men. If we receive repeated recognition and praise over time, we must learn to guard against the temptation to take too much pride in our accomplishments, because pride can easily lead to our downfall.

King Nebuchadnezzar, written about in the Old Testament, was a man who became intensely prideful because of his accomplishments. His pride led him to being judged by God.

Nebuchadnezzar held "the longest and most powerful reign of any monarch in the Neo-Babylonian empire."[8] He reigned from 605 B.C. to 562 B.C. and was ruler over the Babylonians when they attacked the

8 "Nebuchadnezzar II." *Wikipedia.org.* https://en.wikipedia.org/wiki/Nebuchadnezzar_II.

nation of Judah and carried into captivity many of Jerusalem's most influential and gifted citizens.

The book of Daniel begins with a historical account of King Nebuchadnezzar's siege of Jerusalem.

> *During the third year of King Jehoiakim's reign in Judah, King Nebuchadnezzar of Babylon came to Jerusalem and besieged it. The Lord gave him victory over King Jehoiakim of Judah and permitted him to take some of the sacred objects from the Temple of God. So Nebuchadnezzar took them back to the land of Babylonia and placed them in the treasure-house of his god.*
>
> (Daniel 1:1-2)

Prior to his conquest of Jerusalem, King Nebuchadnezzar had successfully conquered the reigning world power of Assyria and definitively ended the attempted uprising of Egypt in the Battle of Carchemish.[9] Nebuchadnezzar's Babylonian reign was one of both power and great accomplishment.

The advancement of architectural beauty was among Nebuchadnezzar's many accomplishments. He was known for constructing palaces, temples, and the Hanging Gardens of Babylon, which is considered one of the Seven Wonders of the Ancient World. John F. Walvoord, longtime president of Dallas Theological Seminary and prominent scholar, described Nebuchadnezzar's building accomplishments and spoke to the king's pride in them:

> The city of Babylon itself... was regarded as the symbol of his power and majesty; and he spared no expense or effort to make it the most beautiful city of the world. If the construction of a great city, magnificent in size,

9 Jeremiah 46:1-12.

> architecture, parks, and armaments, was a proper basis for pride, Nebuchadnezzar was justified.[10]

Of course, to God, there is no good reason to have a prideful heart. Nebuchadnezzar's pride in his architectural achievements became a truly negative force within him, and indeed led him to be judged by God. But that judgment itself led to a remarkable transformation.

Among all the historical records we have in the Old Testament, the story of Nebuchadnezzar's judgment and transformation at the hand of God contains one of the most powerful examples of God's grace.

Just prior to the events that led to King Nebuchadnezzar's transformation, he *"was taking a walk on the flat roof of the royal palace in Babylon. As he looked out across the city, he said, 'Look at this great city of Babylon! By my own mighty power, I have built this beautiful city as my royal residence to display my majestic splendor'"* (Daniel 4:29-30).

Clearly, Nebuchadnezzar saw his accomplishments as evidence of his own greatness. But God chose to use King Nebuchadnezzar's giftings, positional power, and influence for *His own* glory. God took action against the king's pride, and although the action He took was harsh, it also ended up revealing His amazing grace. The story of Nebuchadnezzar's grace-filled transformation is made clear in chapter four of the book of Daniel.

One night, Nebuchadnezzar had a deeply disturbing dream about a tree. The prophet Daniel, one of God's chosen vessels—who lived in exile in Babylon during Nebuchadnezzar's rule over Judah—interpreted the king's dream.

Daniel came before the king and said to him:

> *The tree you saw was growing very tall and strong, reaching high into the heavens for all the world to see. It had fresh green leaves and was loaded with fruit for all to eat. Wild animals lived in its shade, and birds nested in its branches.*

10 From the series: *Daniel The Key to Prophetic Revelation, 4. Nebuchadnezzar's Pride and Punishment*, by John F. Walvoord, https://bible.org/seriespage/4-nebuchadnezzar-s-pride-and-punishment.

That tree, Your Majesty, is you. For you have grown strong and great; your greatness reaches up to heaven, and your rule to the ends of the earth.

Then you saw a messenger, a holy one, coming down from heaven and saying, "Cut down the tree and destroy it. But leave the stump and the roots in the ground, bound with a band of iron and bronze and surrounded by tender grass. Let him be drenched with the dew of heaven. Let him live with the animals of the field for seven periods of time."

This is what the dream means, Your Majesty, and what the Most High has declared will happen to my lord the king. You will be driven from human society, and you will live in the fields with the wild animals. You will eat grass like a cow, and you will be drenched with the dew of heaven.

Seven periods of time will pass while you live this way, until you learn that the Most High rules over the kingdoms of the world and gives them to anyone he chooses.
(Daniel 4:20-25)

At this point, we might choose to look at the sentence pronounced over Nebuchadnezzar's life as simply an example of autocratic dominance—imposing a cruel punishment for human boasting. But by taking that view, we would neglect the grace shown within the acts of our loving God, who will go to whatever lengths necessary to reveal himself to humanity as He truly is—the God of both justice *and* mercy.

Redeeming love pushes past our pride in order to allow God to reveal himself to us.

Pride is one of the greatest weaknesses of the human heart. Our ability to correctly view God's person and position is inevitably skewed when we are exalted in our own eyes. God doesn't want our minds to be clouded by pride. In His graciousness toward us, He combats it in ways that encourage us to learn and possess humility.

In the book of Proverbs, Solomon reminds us of the seriousness of a prideful heart:

> *The Lord detests the proud; they will surely be punished*
> (Proverbs 16:5)

> *Pride goes before destruction, and haughtiness before a fall.*
> (Proverbs 16:18)

> *Pride leads to disgrace, but with humility comes wisdom.*
> (Proverbs 11:2)

God reveals to us through His Word that He does not tolerate a proud heart. Because of his pride, King Nebuchadnezzar was going to learn an important lesson in humility.

Nebuchadnezzar had to learn to humble himself before God.

Daniel's interpretation proved true. Nebuchadnezzar became insane, and he was driven from the palace. He lived in a field like a wild animal. He ate grass like a cow. Since the Bible says his sojourn in the field was long enough for his hair to grow "as long as eagles' feathers," and his nails grew to be like "birds' claws,"[11] the "seven periods of time" from Nebuchadnezzar's vision were likely seven years.[12]

God's grace brought Nebuchadnezzar to the place where he could learn a life-changing lesson. But it took God's judgment to teach him his lesson, and learning it was hard.

We need to adopt an attitude of humility too! We can either succumb to man's fallen nature—be consumed with pride in what we have

11 Daniel 4:33.

12 As translated from the oldest known texts of the Old Testament, the phrase, "seven periods of time," has been most often interpreted as seven years. However, there is some disagreement on the part of scholars on the issue.

accomplished—or we can rise above it, choose God's ways, yield in obedience to God's wisdom, and learn humility.

Hopefully, we will learn to adopt attitudes of humility without so much trouble.

ଔ ଓ

After a long period of time, Nebuchadnezzar's mind was restored, and he was reinstated to the throne. As I retrace in Scripture King Nebuchadnezzar's path of rising in pride, being brought low by God, and then being healed, I am absolutely amazed by the evidence of God's grace in Nebuchadnezzar's restoration. Here are Nebuchadnezzar's own words describing the results:

> *After this time had passed, I, Nebuchadnezzar, looked up to heaven. My sanity returned, and I praised and worshiped the Most High and honored the one who lives forever. His rule is everlasting, and his kingdom is eternal.*
>
> *. . . When my sanity returned to me, so did my honor and glory and kingdom. My advisers and nobles sought me out, and I was restored as head of my kingdom,* ***with even greater honor than before.***
>
> *Now I, Nebuchadnezzar, praise and glorify and honor the King of heaven. All his acts are just and true, and he is able to humble the proud.*
>
> (Daniel 4:34-37, emphasis mine)

How gracious God is! King Nebuchadnezzar not only received back his sanity but also his kingdom. And with that kingdom, he received "*even greater honor than before.*" That was certainly God's grace on display—and Nebuchadnezzar's proclamation of God's greatness reflects his gratitude for it.

> *King Nebuchadnezzar sent this message to the people of every race and nation and language throughout the world:*
>
> *"Peace and prosperity to you!*
>
> *"I want you all to know about the miraculous signs and wonders the Most High God has performed for me. How great are his signs, how powerful his wonders! His kingdom will last forever, his rule through all generations."*
>
> (Daniel 4:1-3)

ɞ ɞ

Each time I read about Nebuchadnezzar's experience, I'm amazed that God didn't simply strike Nebuchadnezzar dead because of his prideful heart. Yet as I type these words, I'm reminded that *all* pride is an affront to God. When it comes to pride, our spiritual responsibilities before God are no different than Nebuchadnezzar's.

Pride working in our hearts can also lead *us* into needing a lesson in humility.

Since the fall of man in the Garden of Eden, the flesh has set itself against the ways of God in every respect. The lust of the flesh drives people toward possessing more and more. Pride over what they have accumulated—be it fame, fortune, power, or anything else that drives them—leads people to trust in their abilities to choose their own paths in life, instead of walking in God's way.

In the book of Proverbs, King Solomon addresses this errant thought.

> *There is a path before each person that seems right, but it ends in death.* (Proverbs 14:12)

Our choice to yield to God everything we take pride in—including our opinions, strengths, and our ability to order our own lives—will prepare us for walking on the path God has determined for us. Our decision to lay down our pride and make pleasing God our first priority exemplifies that we are learning true humility.

The apostle John writes the following in his letter to fellow believers:

> *For the world offers only a craving for physical pleasure, a craving for everything we see, and pride in our achievements and possessions. These are not from the Father, but are from this world. And this world is fading away, along with everything that people crave. But anyone who does what pleases God will live forever.*
>
> (1 John 2:16-17)

Left to follow our own desires, we crave what the world has to offer and fall prey to taking pride in what we have gained in our pursuit of things. But if we reject such pride—if we refuse to follow after the accolades of men and decline to settle for the transient nature of what the world offers—we will please God. When we have the courage to take such a stand, God's grace propels us to a level of living that we could not have otherwise experienced.

King Nebuchadnezzar experienced God's incredible grace. He'd previously spoken boastfully, as if he himself were a god. He attributed all his accomplishments to what he had done. But then, he experienced deliverance from an attitude that could have brought him to total destruction.

And it was only because of grace!

King Nebuchadnezzar's pride was leading him toward certain ruin. It was just a matter of time before he ended up like so many other prideful people whose judgment and violent demise is recorded in Scripture. But God's grace stepped in. God's grace went to work. After coming to his senses, instead of responding to God with anger and accusation, Nebuchadnezzar made a wise choice. He chose to learn his lesson.

Then, praise and words of honor for the "King of heaven" came from the same mouth that had previously spoken prideful boasts. Worth special note is the fact that Nebuchadnezzar uttered those words officially and openly before all nations. His transformation became clear evidence to everyone of the reality of God's grace.

God receives much glory through transformed lives. The life of Nebuchadnezzar certainly was one of those.

☙ ❧

As demonstrated through Nebuchadnezzar's experience, a transformative moment in our lives can provide evidence of God's beautiful grace to those watching. I remember one such moment of transformation in my own life.

I used to enter our church building on the weekends ready to accomplish the many tasks assigned to me as a servant-minded leader. But I was almost oblivious to the reason behind those tasks—to minister to people. Although I marched forward carrying out the tasks before me, I walked right past the people God assigned me to care for. I was completely missing the point of servanthood. Looking back now, I understand that my feelings of self-importance were propelling me toward relational destruction. The Holy Spirit stopped me mid-stride one Sunday morning and said, "Slow down and notice the people around you. Look them in the eye and smile."

I took His admonishment seriously and changed the way I entered and walked through the building. As I began following the Lord's instructions, I realized I was actually being delivered from pride that could have led to my downfall as the Lord's representative. That could have happened if I had continued to focus more on the importance of my own work and accomplishments than on the importance of others.

At a slower pace, I began connecting with people and stopping to listen as they spoke. The most amazing thing happened because of my intentional shift in thinking and action: I fell in love with God's people—my brothers and sisters in Christ. One simple act of obedience was met with a flood of God's grace toward me, and my heart was forever changed.

A woman who had been watching me saw the change in my life, and she told me, "You used to have no time for people, rushing around getting things done. But something changed, and I like you better now."

I share King Nebuchadnezzar's gratitude toward God for delivering me from my own destructive path. The evidence of God's grace on display in my life speaks to others. Undoubtedly, the Lord wants to communicate to others the grace that He is even now imparting to us as He continues teaching us humility and saving us from pride.

As we humble ourselves before God, His grace—His gift of undeserved kindness extended to us—becomes our deliverance from the sure destruction of prideful hearts.

King Nebuchadnezzar foolishly pointed to all his accomplishments as trophies. But in the end, his own life became a witness not to *his* greatness but instead to the greatness of God's grace.

Many are those who—like King Nebuchadnezzar, and like me—have been delivered from pride to testify to God's grace. And we all should be forever grateful for such a beautiful gift.

CHAPTER 3

From Death to Life

MOST EVERYONE I know enjoys receiving gifts. I love Christmas, and unwrapping gifts is one of my favorite activities of the season. One Christmas not long ago, my husband gave me a gift he thought I'd be pleased to receive. I eagerly tore off the wrapping paper after my husband laid his carefully-chosen gift in my hands.

Normally, I would have guessed the contents before I managed to get the wrapping paper off, but this gift puzzled me. Its odd shape and unexpected light weight kept me guessing as I removed the last of the paper and tape.

I sat cross-legged on the floor, inquisitively turning the black-and-gray hexagonal object. I had no idea what it was or what it was supposed to do. My husband's childlike anticipation of my joy faded into unmistakable disappointment as he watched my expressionless face.

Although I recognized his disappointment and wanted to show my appreciation, I simply didn't know what to say. Showing gratitude for a gift—wanted or unwanted—has always been one of my mannerly practices, so my lack of response brought awkward silence into the room. Looking up into my husband's eyes, I timidly asked, "What is it?"

He began to explain that it was a wireless speaker to which my smartphone would connect. "You will be able to listen to music from your phone on it."

I was able to better express my gratitude once I understood the function of the object I held in my hands.

Sometimes, as I read the Word of God, I also feel as if I am unwrapping a gift I don't fully understand. At times, I am challenged by the way God graciously, step by step, reveals Himself to us through His Word.

As I read about the life of Christ in the books of the New Testament, I can imagine that Christ's disciples sometimes felt a similar lack of understanding as Jesus revealed aspects of His nature they had not yet encountered.

The Gospel of the apostle John gives us a compelling record of how the disciples received revelations into the nature of Christ. John wrote his gospel account with the purpose of proving Christ's deity, so that those who read it might believe that Jesus is truly the Son of God.[13] John used Christ's spoken words to point to His deity, and he also recorded miracles performed by Christ during His physical ministry on earth—miracles through which Jesus revealed Himself and backed up His statements in powerful ways.

John recorded the following assertions made by Jesus:

1) *I am the bread of life.* (John 6:35; see also v. 48, & 51)[14]

2) I am the light of the world. (John 9:5; see also 8:12)[15]

3) I am the gate for the sheep. (John 10:7; see also v. 9)[16]

13 "The disciples saw Jesus do many other miraculous signs in addition to the ones recorded in this book. But these are written so that you may continue to believe that Jesus is the Messiah, the Son of God, and that by believing in him you will have life by the power of his name" (John 20:30-31).

14 Jesus spoke this in the context of the feeding of the five thousand recorded in John 6.

15 Jesus spoke this in the context of His healing of the man born blind recorded in John 9:1-7. He brought light to the eyes of the blind man. Following this miracle, Jesus went on to speak about spiritual blindness.

16 Jesus spoke of being the "gate for the sheep" as part of His response to the Pharisees who were questioning the healing of the blind man. This is part of Jesus' discourse about spiritual blindness—still in context with,

4) I am the good shepherd. (John 10:11, 14)[17]

5) I am the resurrection and the life. (John 11:25)[18]

6) I am the way, the truth, and the life. (John 14:6)[19]

7) I am the true grapevine. (John 15:1)[20]

These claims made by Jesus during His earthly ministry have been aptly named the seven "I am" statements.

In the Old Testament book of Exodus, it is recorded that God chose Moses to lead the children of Israel out of Egypt. Moses asked God to tell him what he should say when the people questioned his authority.

> *But Moses protested, "If I go to the people of Israel and tell them, 'The God of your ancestors has sent me to you,' they will ask me, 'What is his name?' Then what should I tell them?"*
>
> *God replied to Moses, "I Am who I Am. Say this to the people of Israel: I Am has sent me to you."*
>
> (Exodus 3:13-14)

Just as God used "I Am" to describe himself to Moses and the children of Israel in the Old Testament, Jesus described himself as "I Am" in the New Testament to confirm His identity, purpose, and authority.

---

and as a result of, the healing of the blind man. In the last part of chapter 9 through the first part of chapter 10, He draws a contrast between Himself—the gate for the sheep—and the Pharisees, who are not only spiritually blind but also thieves and robbers—those who don't go through "the gate" but instead sneak over the wall of the sheepfold.

17 Jesus spoke of being *"the good shepherd"* following His statement of being "*the gate for the sheep.*" See the above footnote.

18 This was spoken in the context of Jesus raising Lazarus from the dead.

19 During the Last Supper, Jesus told the disciples He was going away, and said, *"And you know the way to where I am going"* (John 14:4). Following that, Thomas asked, *"How can we know the way?"* Jesus told them He *is* "the Way."

20 This was also spoken by Jesus at the Last Supper, as part of His final words to His disciples before His arrest and crucifixion.

Throughout his gospel, John tells us that Christ came in contact with the powers of darkness and overcame each one personally—through the life He lived and in the way He ministered to others. How wonderful that God reveals His nature and power to us through His Son, Jesus Christ! These revelations allow us to observe and benefit from the change wrought in people's lives by the demonstrations of God's power and wonderful grace.

☙ ❧

One recipient of God's gracious and powerful touch was Lazarus, brother of Mary and Martha and friend of Jesus. Because Lazarus' story is recorded in Scripture, we have the benefit of a front-row seat from which to view God's grace manifested through it. John records the evidence of Jesus' identity as the Resurrection and the Life through the story of Lazarus.

> *A man named Lazarus was sick. He lived in Bethany with his sisters, Mary and Martha. This is the Mary who later poured the expensive perfume on the Lord's feet and wiped them with her hair. Her brother, Lazarus, was sick. So the two sisters sent a message to Jesus telling him, "Lord, your dear friend is very sick."* (John 11:1-3)

Sickness was consuming Lazarus' body, and he was near death. The power of Jesus to heal was well known, and both Mary and Martha knew it was time to call Jesus. Jesus was the one who would come to their home and heal their brother.

> *But when Jesus heard about it he said, "Lazarus's sickness will not end in death. No, it happened for the glory of God so that the Son of God will receive glory from this." So although Jesus loved Martha, Mary, and Lazarus, he stayed where he was for the next two days.*
>
> (John 11:4-6)

And Lazarus died.

One might understand if the disciples were feeling confused when, two days after Jesus told them Lazarus' sickness would "not end in death," He told them it was time to go to Bethany because Lazarus was dead.[21]

But they knew the words of Jesus were dependable. When Jesus spoke, He always spoke the truth. They had been learning by experience that Jesus was always right. Could Jesus have lied to them? Jesus appeared to have told them one thing; then, two days later, He told them something contradictory.

It may have appeared that, for the first time, Jesus showed that He could be wrong—that He failed. But of course, we know this wasn't the case. Lazarus' sickness may have involved death, but, just as Jesus said, it didn't end in death. In fact, it ended in life in a way the disciples and others didn't expect.

Jesus had a grace-filled plan, and He was carrying it out.

Jesus and the disciples began their journey to the region of Judea. Upon their arrival in Bethany, they learned that Lazarus had already been in the grave four days—something Jesus knew but had not told His disciples.

> *When Martha got word that Jesus was coming, she went to meet him. But Mary stayed in the house. Martha said to Jesus, "Lord, if only you had been here, my brother would not have died. But even now I know that God will give you whatever you ask."*
>
> *Jesus told her, "Your brother will rise again."*
>
> *"Yes," Martha said, "he will rise when everyone else rises, at the last day."*

21 John 11:7-15.

> *Jesus told her, "I am the resurrection and the life. Anyone who believes in me will live, even after dying. Everyone who lives in me and believes in me will never ever die. Do you believe this, Martha?"* (John 11:20-26)

Although they already knew Jesus had power to bring to life one who had died, [22] no one expected Jesus to raise Lazarus from the dead. He had been dead too long.

But Jesus had set the stage to reveal himself not just as "the resurrection and the life" someday in the future, but that day—in their moment of need. Arriving at Lazarus' tomb, Jesus demonstrated His power over death and spoke words of life.

> *"Roll the stone aside," Jesus told them.*
>
> *But Martha, the dead man's sister, protested, "Lord, he has been dead for four days. The smell will be terrible."*
>
> *Jesus responded, "Didn't I tell you that you would see God's glory if you believe?"*
>
> *So they rolled the stone aside. Then Jesus looked up to heaven and said, "Father, thank you for hearing me. You always hear me, but I said it out loud for the sake of all these people standing here, so that they will believe you sent me."*
>
> *Then Jesus shouted, "Lazarus, come out!"*
>
> *And the dead man came out, his hands and feet bound in graveclothes, his face wrapped in a headcloth.*

22 It appears that Lazarus was raised from the dead shortly before Christ's crucifixion. Jesus had already raised at least two others from the dead earlier in His ministry, but no one had been raised who had been dead as long as Lazarus. The widow of Nain's son was raised from the dead during his funeral procession (Luke 7:11-17), and the people of the Middle East buried their dead quickly, without embalming the body. Jesus raised Jairus' daughter from the dead just after she died—while her body was still lying on her bed (Matthew 9:18-23; Mark 5:35-43).

Jesus told them, "Unwrap him and let him go!"
(John 11:39-44)

Lazarus received his life back—he was restored to health, freed from the grip of death. What a beautiful gift of grace! It was a gift not only for Lazarus but also for the disciples and the others who witnessed it—and for all of those who have read the story since then, including us.

Jesus' command, "Unwrap him and let him go!" sealed and proclaimed His authority over the most formidable opponent of human existence—death. Yes, Jesus proved His claim and showed that even death stands powerless before our Lord.

In our lives, we may encounter not only the death of a loved one but also the death of dreams, relationships, or expectations. The pain associated with those things can overwhelm us and tempt us to wonder if God will become our resurrection of hope and new life in the midst of what seems so utterly destroyed.

Wrapped in our pain, we yearn to hear the voice of our Lord say for us also, "Unwrap him and let him go!"

He can, of course. If He can raise the dead and give new life to a person who has been in the grave long enough to begin to decay, it is no challenge for Him to speak life to any circumstance in which we find ourselves. But He not only can, He will—if we'll simply trust Him to do it. Just as Jesus called, "Lazarus, come out!" so will He call us out of our most painful moments into new life.

Mary, Martha, and Lazarus experienced God's grace first-hand as Jesus brought life from death. Jesus is also offering us the opportunity to experience God's grace. As we bring our pain and devastation to Him, He breathes newness of life into our hearts and our situations. Grace—the gift of undeserved kindness—is granted to us by the One who has complete authority over death itself.

Just as I was puzzled over the Christmas gift I turned about in my hands, we can be puzzled over the experiences we have in our lives. We can wonder about God's purpose in allowing us to experience things, and we can be puzzled over why God handles things the way He does.

But the Lord sustains us through all our challenges, and we receive such blessings once He reveals His plan.

I am overwhelmed and astonished by the kindness of God, who extends such grace to us.

☙ ❧

The apostle John experienced a revelation from Christ while he was exiled on the island of Patmos near the end of his life. John was given a vision, and the Lord instructed him to write down what he saw and send it to the seven churches in the province of Asia.[23]

What John recorded is what we know today as the New Testament book of Revelation. In John's account of his revelation experience, we get a glimpse of his encounter with Christ.

John describes what he saw:

> *His head and his hair were white like wool, as white as snow. And his eyes were like flames of fire. His feet were like polished bronze refined in a furnace, and his voice thundered like mighty ocean waves. He held seven stars in his right hand, and a sharp two-edged sword came from his mouth. And his face was like the sun in all its brilliance.*
>
> *When I saw him, I fell at his feet as if I were dead. But he laid his right hand on me and said, "Don't be afraid! I am the First and the Last. I am the living one. I died, but look—I am alive forever and ever! And I hold the keys of death and the grave.* (Revelation 1:14-18)

John had experienced Jesus as the Son of Man when they walked together for three years. John had also experienced Jesus as the Son of

23 Revelation 1:9-11.

God when He raised Lazarus from the dead, and when He conquered death through His own resurrection on the third day.

Through the revelation he received on the island of Patmos, John experienced even more of the reality of God's eternal plan and power when he saw a vision of Christ in His glory and heard Jesus once again declare, "I am!"

Death has been forever vanquished by the great I Am! Jesus declared that He is the resurrection and the life. He is true Life. We will one day pass from this earth into eternal life with Christ. But today, as we continue to live on earth, He is our Life even now—the Life that provides us the grace we need in our difficulties and seemingly hopeless situations.

Lazarus stands in history as a trophy of what God can accomplish even in the face of complete hopelessness. The resurrection of Lazarus, and the many other ways in which God has demonstrated His ability to bring life from death—both physically and spiritually—stand as undeniable proof of God's timeless and continuing grace.

Having personally experienced how God has spoken life into so many circumstances during my own lifetime, I can fully express my thankfulness to Him for His wonderful gift of grace. Our wonderful Lord continually stands ready to extend to us His grace and move us and our circumstances from death to life.

CHAPTER 4

A MATTER OF TRUST

ALTHOUGH WE MAY mentally agree that we have access to forgiveness, healing, love, restoration, and many other things God has provided for us through His grace, appropriating them into our lives is often more challenging than simply acknowledging they exist.

I contend that appropriating these gifts and God's promises almost always requires that we move beyond our understanding of what exists in the physical realm to accept what God says exists in the spiritual realm. And because our fleshly minds often battle against us, that process can sometimes seem elusive.

For instance, we accept and believe that God's Word says we can be healed from any disease.[24] But when we receive a diagnosis from

24 "These miraculous signs will accompany those who believe: They will cast out demons in my name, and they will speak in new languages. They will be able to handle snakes with safety, and if they drink anything poisonous, it won't hurt them. They will be able to place their hands on the sick, and they will be healed" (Mark 16:17-18).

"Are any of you sick? You should call for the elders of the church to come and pray over you, anointing you with oil in the name of the Lord. Such a prayer offered in faith will heal the sick, and the Lord will make you well. And if you have committed any sins, you will be forgiven" (James 5:14-15).

the doctor that matter-of-factly states we have a disease, moving from accepting the diagnosis to appropriating healing may be challenging for us.

We need a solution for that, and I like to put the solution this way: we must trade the reality of the doctor's report for the promise in God's Word.

To me, this action of trading what currently exists for what God says we can have is the essence of trust.

Trust tends to be the natural outcome of a relationship built on the foundation of faithful consistency over time—not only in thought but also in action. When we speak of our ability to exhibit trust in God to fulfill His promises, we're drawing on trust developed over time, because He has proven Himself faithful over and over again.

In many ways, the trust relationship we have with God is unlike our relationships with our fellow man. We develop a basic level of trust with one another, knowing that we are, at some point, going to fail each other because of our sinful, human nature. But God cannot fail. God cannot be unfaithful to us. So when we trust in God, it is like trusting in no other. When we trust God, we trust One who is sovereign and wholly unlike us when it comes to dependability.

God's sovereignty and faithfulness provide for us a gracious relationship worthy of our complete trust. What we learn of His faithfulness inspires us to trust in things unseen—things yet to be received.

Believing in what is unseen—which can sometimes be difficult even for Christians—requires that we have complete trust in not only what the Bible says but also in our faithful God, who gives it to us.

We willingly and readily say that we believe in God. But although we attend church and sing of His greatness and limitless power, do we truly trust Him and His ability to do great, seemingly impossible exploits in and through our lives?

Many people have been faced with the spirit of this question. Without perhaps actually saying it in these words, people have had to

---

"Yet it was our weaknesses he carried; it was our sorrows that weighed him down. And we thought his troubles were a punishment from God, a punishment for his own sins! But he was pierced for our rebellion, crushed for our sins. He was beaten so we could be whole. He was whipped so we could be healed" (Isaiah 53:4-5).

ask themselves, "Do I accept my current reality or trade it for what God says in His Word that I can have?"

ᏇᎦ ᏕᏍ

I'm drawn to a story in the New Testament in which a man is faced with the stark reality and finality of the death of his daughter. The man's name is Jairus.

Jairus was a leader of the local synagogue in Capernaum. His daughter was terribly ill and dying, and he went to Jesus. Believing that the reality of his daughter's sickness could be reversed—bringing healing to her body—he asked Jesus to intervene. In Jairus' own words, we see evidence of his trust in the ability of Jesus to heal.

> *Then a leader of the local synagogue, whose name was Jairus, arrived. When he saw Jesus, he fell at his feet, pleading fervently with him. "My little daughter is dying," he said. "Please come and lay your hands on her; heal her so she can live."*
>
> *Jesus went with him, and all the people followed, crowding around him.* (Mark 5:22-24)

Jairus trusted that Jesus could change the outcome of his little girl's diagnosis. And Jairus surely must have felt relief when Jesus agreed to go with him. But as Jairus and Jesus traveled together, they were pressed on every side by the crowd surrounding Jesus. From within the crowd, another person who sought Jesus' touch reached out to Him.

> *A woman in the crowd had suffered for twelve years with constant bleeding. She had suffered a great deal from many doctors, and over the years she had spent everything she had to pay them, but she had gotten no better. In fact, she had gotten worse.*

She had heard about Jesus, so she came up behind him through the crowd and touched his robe. For she thought to herself, "If I can just touch his robe, I will be healed."

Immediately the bleeding stopped, and she could feel in her body that she had been healed of her terrible condition.

Jesus realized at once that healing power had gone out from him, so he turned around in the crowd and asked, "Who touched my robe?"

His disciples said to him, "Look at this crowd pressing around you. How can you ask, 'Who touched me?'"

But he kept on looking around to see who had done it. Then the frightened woman, trembling at the realization of what had happened to her, came and fell to her knees in front of him and told him what she had done.

And he said to her, "Daughter, your faith has made you well. Go in peace. Your suffering is over." (Mark 5:25-34)

It would be natural to assume that these two stories are unrelated, but nothing in Scripture is without purpose. We would be wise to view the stories as intertwined—Jairus was impacted in at least some way by the event of the woman's healing. Jairus saw the healing power of Jesus displayed, so surely his trust in Christ's ability to heal his daughter increased in that moment.

☙ ❧

As I consider the story of Jairus and his daughter, I am reminded of a visit I made one day to a pediatrician's office with my son when he was about thirteen years old. In order to play school sports, each participant was required to have an annual sports physical. So we scheduled and kept the necessary appointment, as we did each year.

As the pediatrician examined my son's spine, she commented that it was unusually curved. She went so far as to say she believed he had scoliosis.

In that very moment, I searched inwardly for reassurance from God and initiated a quiet conversation with the Holy Spirit. Once my spirit had settled into His peace, I knew my son's diagnosis would be changed by the One in whom I had learned to trust. Recalling the many other times I had seen God's healing intervention in my children's lives, I trusted that He would provide the needed healing this time, as well.

I trusted God and went to Him to heal my son.

The pediatrician ordered a full set of x-rays to be taken of my son's back at the local children's hospital, and she strongly urged us to keep the appointment. We arrived and sat in the waiting room with children who wore back braces and walked with various assistive devices.

I admit that my courage wavered as I looked around the waiting room and saw the physical realities of the other children and their parents. My compassion for them was great, and what I saw presented a challenge to my faith, but I chose to trust that my son's diagnosis would result in healing, not in corrective care.

After many x-rays were taken, the doctor came into our examination room. His first question was, "Did one of the nurses at your pediatrician's office order these x-rays?"

With some confusion, I responded, "No, the pediatrician herself ordered the x-rays."

He proceeded to explain that he could not understand why anyone would have requested these x-rays on my son's back. He said, "Your son's spine could not be more perfect."

My heart rejoiced over both the doctor's words and God's gracious gift of healing. I knew God had touched my son and healed him! Similarly to the response of the woman who was healed when she touched Jesus' robe, my heart was full of gratitude for Christ's grace-filled healing of my son.

My trust in God for my son's health was challenged by unwelcome, unavoidable, physical realities around me, but I traded all of them for the reality of God's promises and healing that continue to exist in the spiritual realm.

However, as for the challenges Jairus faced, they were soon to get tougher than the one I faced that day. Even as his faith and expectation for his daughter's healing were increasing, Jairus received news that his daughter had died.

> *While [Jesus] was still speaking to her, messengers arrived from the home of Jairus, the leader of the synagogue. They told him, "Your daughter is dead. There's no use troubling the Teacher now."* (Mark 5:35)

It's hard for me to imagine how devastated Jairus must have felt when he heard the news. He had put his trust in Jesus to heal his daughter, and then, in an agonizing moment of conflict, Jairus must have yearned for strength to bear up against the new reality that was facing him.

But Jesus, the Healer, was still with him. And in His graciousness, Jesus reassured Jairus. In hindsight, we can see that Jesus was letting Jairus know that nothing had changed in the spiritual realm. Without actually saying so, Jesus was intimating that the healing Jairus sought for his daughter was still available.

> *But Jesus overheard them and said to Jairus, "Don't be afraid. Just have faith."* (Mark 5:36)

We can hope that a renewed trust in Jesus was birthed within Jairus after Jesus spoke to him. That was clearly Christ's intention. But knowing all too well human weaknesses and tendencies, one doesn't have to imagine too much to believe Jairus was still challenged to look beyond the physical realities he was facing.

I can only wonder what was going through Jairus' mind as Jesus accompanied him the rest of the way to his home. Nevertheless, he surely received at least some encouragement by what Jesus did next.

Jesus stopped the crowd from following Him on the rest of His journey. Attempting to put myself in the shoes of Jairus at that moment, I believe I would have received both comfort and hope from knowing Jesus was shutting out distractions and focusing only on my need.

> *Then Jesus stopped the crowd and wouldn't let anyone go with him except Peter, James, and John (the brother of James). When they came to the home of the synagogue leader, Jesus saw much commotion and weeping and wailing. He went inside and asked, "Why all this commotion and weeping? The child isn't dead; she's only asleep."*
>
> *The crowd laughed at him. But he made them all leave, and he took the girl's father and mother and his three disciples into the room where the girl was lying.*
>
> (Mark 5:37-40)

Separating ourselves from the commotion of the crowd in times of difficulty can enable us to focus and maintain trust that God will bring answers and solutions to us.

I experienced such a need for separation several years ago, when I was visiting a friend in the hospital. My friend Christy had been battling cancer and was nearing the end of her fight. Her family had been called in to say their last goodbyes, and Christy asked me to join them.

As I entered, I sensed an urgency to clear the room and pray. Since I was not a family member, it would have been a bit awkward to ask everyone to leave, so I inwardly prayed that God would clear the room for me.

One by one, family members decided to go to the cafeteria or to get coffee, until the only ones remaining in the room were Christy, her brother, and me.

I looked at Christy's brother, told him I was about to pray, and asked if he'd like to stay. What happened next totally surprised me. He said that, even though he didn't know how to pray, he wanted to stay. I sensed that he wanted to place his trust in the saving power of Christ—and indeed he did! I had the privilege of leading her brother into the presence of Jesus, and he became a Christian that day. Christy and I were overjoyed!

The healing that was applied in Christy's hospital room that day was complete, but it was spiritual rather than physical. We held Christy's funeral a short time later. It was a beautiful celebration of her life. As the family was following the casket out of the church, Christy's brother stepped out of the line, wrapped his arms around me, and thanked me for leading him to Christ.

His spiritual healing was complete on earth, just as Christy's healing had been made complete in Heaven.

What beautiful, saving, and healing grace!

☙ ❧

It would have been completely and utterly noteworthy—still well worth Mark's time to record—if Jesus had brought only salvation on earth and future hope to Jairus' family and loved ones. But Jesus used the occasion not only to display God's grace and mercy for sinners, but also to prove that the trust we put in Him for physical healing is well-deserved.

As Jesus entered the room where the girl was lying, Jairus was about to experience a previously unexpected work of God's grace. Although we read that Jesus told Jairus and others that the child wasn't dead but only asleep, it isn't clear that anyone aside from Jesus' disciples actually expected what was to come next.[25]

Jesus wasn't simply making a theological statement about death being a temporary state where the flesh and spirit are separated until the resurrection.[26] He was about to prove it.

25 Peter, James, and John already knew of Christ's power to raise the dead. They were aware of the first time Jesus raised the dead—the son of the widow of Nain. That miracle is recorded in Luke 7:11-17.

26 This could have been the synagogue leader's initial understanding of Jesus' words because of his relationship with theology. And that would be consistent with what Martha thought Jesus was talking about when Jesus told her Lazarus would rise again. See John 11:17-26.

> *Holding her hand, he said to her, "Talitha koum," which means "Little girl, get up!" And the girl, who was twelve years old, immediately stood up and walked around! They were overwhelmed and totally amazed.*
>
> (Mark 5:41-42)

The lives of the girl's mother and father, and the crowd that had originally laughed at Jesus, had to have been changed by the gift of healing grace they experienced that day. Jesus proved He could be trusted.

After reading about how Christ healed both the woman and Jairus' daughter, we should be encouraged to trust the value of Jesus's admonition to have faith in him while we endure our own challenging experiences in life.

☙ ❧

Jairus' daughter was brought from death to life. The woman who suffered with constant bleeding was healed. My friend Christy was delivered from disease in a way that eternity will one day prove. Christy's brother was miraculously saved through a circumstance only God could have arranged. And my son received a notable healing touch.

All these examples of how God came to the rescue when the chips were down serve to prove that He can be trusted in every way. We all experience God's grace when we exhibit our faith in God and trust Jesus. We need God to move in our lives, and we can experience His grace and have access to the solutions He provides in our times of need as He fulfills His beautiful promises.

But in order for us to trade our sometimes painful and limiting realities in the physical realm for spiritual realities—the ones God desires to reveal in our lives today—we must determine not to allow our faith to be overcome by circumstances. Through every challenge, we can determine in our hearts to depend on God's grace and His ability to change things for our good. By doing so, we position ourselves to receive God's very best as we place our faith in the One who is always faithful.

Believing God, and allowing our lives to become trophies of His grace, is often simply a matter of trust.

CHAPTER 5

More Than Enough

IN OUR TIMES of crisis, we may be tempted to feel like God is far away from, or perhaps uninterested in, what we're going through. We may feel that we desperately need to see evidence of His nearness, His caring, and His intervention. We don't want to go through such times; but it is in these times of difficulty that we can beautifully experience and come to appreciate God's grace like never before.

God's grace is always present with us, whether we're fully aware of it or not. Even in the worst of times, we can depend on God to pour out His grace on us and prove that His love and care is more than enough to take us through every crisis.

As our Creator, God could have chosen long ago to maintain no obligation toward us—to refuse to comfort us or be involved in our lives. But He has revealed in His Word—and He has proven over and over to us through His interactions with mankind throughout history—that He made the opposite choice.

As we read God's Word, we are constantly reminded that He desires to be near us, care for us, and intervene on our behalf. As do parents who love their children, God watches over our lives to help us grow in maturity and bless us with good things.

Note just a few Scriptures that illustrate God's continuing involvement in our lives:

> *For God has said, "I will never fail you. I will never abandon you."* (Hebrews 13:5)

> *Once I was young, and now I am old. Yet I have never seen the godly abandoned or their children begging for bread.* (Psalm 37:25)

> *And I will ask the Father, and he will give you another Advocate, who will never leave you.* (John 14:16)

> *The Lord says, "I will rescue those who love me. I will protect those who trust in my name."* (Psalm 91:14)

But even with the assurances of Scripture, when we're experiencing difficulty, it can be challenging to maintain the confidence in God that we feel we have when we're experiencing times of ease. However, if we'll lean into a closer relationship with Him in the bad moments, we'll find that He is more than willing and able to lead us through all of life's challenges.

☙ ❧

The Old Testament contains the record of huge challenges experienced by a man named Job. Today, Job is certainly one of the trophies standing tall in God's grace-filled trophy case.

Job experienced what anyone would call abundance. He was a man who honored God, and God allowed him to accumulate great wealth. I imagine all the people who knew Job felt like he had more than enough in the way of riches. He was indeed greatly blessed by God.

> *There once was a man named Job who lived in the land of Uz. He was blameless—a man of complete integrity. He feared God and stayed away from evil. He had seven sons and three daughters. He owned 7,000 sheep, 3,000 camels, 500 teams of oxen, and 500 female donkeys. He also had many servants. He was, in fact, the richest person in that entire area.* (Job 1:1-3)

Job was wealthy in every way. He was rich when it came to having children, which was a huge blessing.[27] He had great numbers of livestock. And he had many workers to help him care for his holdings. But as we continue reading in the book of Job, we find that the time came when he had to walk through extraordinarily devastating circumstances.

> *One day the members of the heavenly court came to present themselves before the Lord, and the Accuser, Satan, came with them. "Where have you come from?" the Lord asked Satan.*
>
> *Satan answered the Lord, "I have been patrolling the earth, watching everything that's going on."*
>
> *Then the Lord asked Satan, "Have you noticed my servant Job? He is the finest man in all the earth. He is blameless—a man of complete integrity. He fears God and stays away from evil."*
>
> *Satan replied to the Lord, "Yes, but Job has good reason to fear God. You have always put a wall of protection around him and his home and his property. You have made him prosper in everything he does. Look how rich he is! But reach out and take away everything he has, and he will surely curse you to your face!"*

27 "Children born to a young man are like arrows in a warrior's hands. How joyful is the man whose quiver is full of them! He will not be put to shame when he confronts his accusers at the city gates" (Psalm 127:4-5).

> *"All right, you may test him," the Lord said to Satan. "Do whatever you want with everything he possesses, but don't harm him physically." So Satan left the Lord's presence.*
> (Job 1:6-12)

I have to admit that this story has always puzzled me. Why would God offer Job's life for Satan's consideration and attack? I'm not sure I'll know the answer this side of heaven, but knowing the end of Job's story helps me understand how God's grace is revealed in even the worst of circumstances.

As we continue to read Job's story, we find that, because of Job's relationship with God, he not only had more than enough of this world's possessions—he had more than enough of what was even more important: faith and integrity.

God was about to reveal to the world how He honors and rewards those who fully trust in Him. He was about to demonstrate how His restorative abilities are without measure.

There came a time when Job needed God's restorative powers. Before we read of the beauty of God's restorative work in Job's life, we must read about circumstances that brought him to the point of despairing his own life.

Job's faith in God was tested in every way imaginable. The intensity of the testing he faced was fierce—wave after wave of bad news flooded his life.

> *One day when Job's sons and daughters were feasting at the oldest brother's house, a messenger arrived at Job's home with this news: "Your oxen were plowing, with the donkeys feeding beside them, when the Sabeans raided us. They stole all the animals and killed all the farmhands. I am the only one who escaped to tell you."*
> (Job 1:13-15)

That day had likely been going along like many others. Job was home, and his children were together at Job's oldest son's house. Imagine Job's shock when he heard not only that all of his oxen and donkeys were stolen, but also that his farmhands had been killed.

Before that news could fully sink in, another messenger arrived.

> *While he was still speaking, another messenger arrived with this news: "The fire of God has fallen from heaven and burned up your sheep and all the shepherds. I am the only one who escaped to tell you."* (Job 1:16)

Fire—likely a severe lightning storm—had consumed Job's sheep and all his shepherds except for the person who carried the news. Job's day had quickly gone from bad to worse, but more bad news was soon to come.

> *While he was still speaking, a third messenger arrived with this news: "Three bands of Chaldean raiders have stolen your camels and killed your servants. I am the only one who escaped to tell you."* (Job 1:17)

Yet a third messenger arrived and told Job that all his camels had been stolen and his servants killed. At this point, Job had lost all of his livestock and all except for a small handful of his servants, farmhands, and workers.

But the worst news was yet to come. A fourth messenger then arrived with this news:

> *"Your sons and daughters were feasting in their oldest brother's home. Suddenly, a powerful wind swept in from the wilderness and hit the house on all sides. The house collapsed, and all your children are dead. I am the only one who escaped to tell you."* (Job 1:18b-19)

It's hard to imagine how devastated Job must have felt as the world around him collapsed. He not only lost his possessions and farm workers—he lost all his children. Perhaps Job's devastation might have justified an incredibly angry response toward God. But God's Word states:

> *In all of this, Job did not sin by blaming God.* (Job 1:22)

Satan's accusation proved to be false! Job's loss did not result in him cursing God. Job had passed the test, but it wouldn't be the last test he had to experience. Satan approached God once again.

> *One day the members of the heavenly court came again to present themselves before the Lord, and the Accuser, Satan, came with them. "Where have you come from?" the Lord asked Satan.*
>
> *Satan answered the Lord, "I have been patrolling the earth, watching everything that's going on."*
>
> *Then the Lord asked Satan, "Have you noticed my servant Job? He is the finest man in all the earth. He is blameless—a man of complete integrity. He fears God and stays away from evil. And he has maintained his integrity, even though you urged me to harm him without cause."*
>
> *Satan replied to the Lord, "Skin for skin! A man will give up everything he has to save his life. But reach out and take away his health, and he will surely curse you to your face!"*
>
> *"All right, do with him as you please," the Lord said to Satan. "But spare his life."*
>
> *So Satan left the Lord's presence, and he struck Job with terrible boils from head to foot.* (Job 2:1-7)

Before—during the first testing—the test of Job's faith and trust in God was limited to the loss of possessions, farmhands, and children with which God had blessed him. Job's own life and health had not been affected. But in the second test, God allowed Satan to challenge Job's relationship with God and his motivation in trusting Him by threatening his life and physical comfort.

Did Job honor God because of God's blessings on his life and his own wellbeing, or did Job honor God because he truly revered Him in spite of all circumstances? That question was certainly at the core of Satan's accusation.

☙ ❧

I suppose we all want to question the Lord about our experiences at some point. In my own reading about Job's experience—and during this particular time in my life, as I write this chapter—there's something inside me that simply wants to ask God why He would allow such intense devastation in a believer's life. The challenges I've dealt with over the years seem to be plenty. But I can't imagine being in the position Job was in.

I don't like my own pain, and I don't like watching others experience pain. But I believe we are learning from Job's experiences—and our own—that trusting God to lead us through the pain-filled questions allows us to be humble before the Lord. And that humility becomes an open conduit through which God's grace powerfully flows.

Several times over the last few days, I have drawn close to my mother's side. For almost four years now, she has valiantly battled Stage 4 cancer in her body. Recently, she also experienced four successive strokes that have left her body weak and exhausted.

As much as I want to see her completely restored to health here on earth, I also know it's a privilege for her to go home to be with the Lord. She's ready to see Jesus, and she longs to be free from fighting illness. Watching my mom's health decline is difficult enough for me, but I'm also watching my dad hold on to her life as tightly as possible each day. My heart hurts to watch him walk through that process.

Dad's faithful marriage partner of fifty-five years stands ready to exchange her earthly life for her heavenly promise. God's promise to both of them is very real. For those who place their faith and trust in God, parting is not forever.

> *For the Lord himself will come down from heaven with a commanding shout, with the voice of the archangel, and with the trumpet call of God. First, the believers who have died will rise from their graves. Then, together with them, we who are still alive and remain on the earth will be caught up in the clouds to meet the Lord in the air. Then we will be with the Lord forever.*
>
> (1 Thessalonians 4:16-17)

As for me, my grief is great, but it's tempered by the beautiful grace my God has poured out upon all of us. He has shown himself to me, over and over again throughout my life, to be the giver of more than enough. And that goes for whatever I have needed in every circumstance. I am finding that humbly enduring the loss of what is precious to us positions us to yet again experience His comforting grace.

☙ ❧

Job lost his health. He became terribly ill. In mourning, he sat in the middle of a heap of ashes, as was customary in that day to signify to others his sorrow. But even through that experience, he showed an attitude of humble endurance and trust in God—even when his wife challenged him to curse God.

> *Job scraped his skin with a piece of broken pottery as he sat among the ashes. His wife said to him, "Are you still trying to maintain your integrity? Curse God and die."*

> *But Job replied, "You talk like a foolish woman. Should we accept only good things from the hand of God and never anything bad?"*
>
> *So in all this, Job said nothing wrong.* (Job 2:8-10)

Perhaps Job's wife endured the loss of Job's children and possessions without making such a rash statement, but she certainly reached her limit when Job became so deathly ill. She allowed herself to become Satan's mouthpiece, trying to convince Job to do what Satan had told God Job would do.

But Job didn't allow his wife's disdain for God to influence his understanding of God's character. For us to hold steady as we walk through our pain, we must maintain our own personal trust in God and our own individual reliance on His character. Not even those who are closest to us can be allowed to dissuade us from continuing to place our faith and trust in God.

Following Job's wife's statement and Job's response, most of the rest of the book is made up of conversations between Job and his friends, who came to visit him. They spoke to him some words of encouragement, but they also made misguided accusations as they tried to reason how such things could befall him.

His friends tried to convince Job that, if he had not offended God, none of the terrible things he experienced would have happened. While Job's words exemplified the struggle we all feel as we grapple with the difficulties of life and cling to faith in the middle of our pain, Job refused to accept blame for his situation.

Toward the end of the book, God finally intervened in the situation. Job's friends were terribly wrong in many of the things they said to Job. While Job was more right than wrong in his response, he also struggled to bring reason to the situation. God finally had heard enough from all of them, and He took over the conversation.

The Lord expressed his disapproval of Job's friends. Even though God stood firmly behind His relationship with Job, He still took action to teach Job further humility by reminding him (and his so-called comforters) of the fact that, in the larger picture, we are all relatively ignorant before God and completely dependent on what He allows.

When God finished speaking to them, Job's response to God was one of seemingly complete humility, with no evidence of self-justification.

> *Then Job replied to the Lord:*
>
> *"I know that you can do anything, and no one can stop you. You asked, 'Who is this that questions my wisdom with such ignorance?' It is I—and I was talking about things I knew nothing about, things far too wonderful for me. You said, 'Listen and I will speak! I have some questions for you, and you must answer them.' I had only heard about you before, but now I have seen you with my own eyes. I take back everything I said, and I sit in dust and ashes to show my repentance."*
>
> (Job 42:1-6)

Nothing is said about Job's friends willingly responding to God in humility. God expressed His anger towards Job's friends, who had mischaracterized God and Job's standing before Him. God demanded that they provide a sacrifice for themselves, and had Job pray for them so they wouldn't receive from God what their actions deserved.

Then, God began to restore to Job what had been lost.

> *When Job prayed for his friends, the Lord restored his fortunes. In fact, the Lord gave him twice as much as before!*
>
> *Then all his brothers, sisters, and former friends came and feasted with him in his home. And they consoled him and comforted him because of all the trials the Lord had brought against him. And each of them brought him a gift of money and a gold ring.*

> *So the Lord blessed Job in the second half of his life even more than in the beginning. For now he had 14,000 sheep, 6,000 camels, 1,000 teams of oxen, and 1,000 female donkeys. He also gave Job seven more sons and three more daughters.*
>
> *He named his first daughter Jemimah, the second Keziah, and the third Keren-happuch. In all the land no women were as lovely as the daughters of Job. And their father put them into his will along with their brothers.*
>
> *Job lived 140 years after that, living to see four generations of his children and grandchildren. Then he died, an old man who had lived a long, full life.*
>
> (Job 42:10-17)

What incredible grace was at work in Job's life! God proved that He can be trusted to care for those who honor Him through every circumstance. God restored to Job not only what others likely considered more than enough, but twice that much.

☙ ❧

Although I would not willingly invite such testing into my own life, I'm grateful that we have the opportunity to witness the beauty of God's restorative and abundant grace as it was applied to Job's life.

Perhaps God allowed Satan's attack on Job to send a powerful message to those of us who have, like Job, placed our future, our trust, in His hands—a message of abundant, overwhelming grace that can be delivered in no other way.

How great God's grace is! Our hardships and difficulties are made bearable knowing that He is present and cares so much for us.

As we humble ourselves before God, and as we determine to hold on to our faith in the Lord, like Job—who became one of the greatest trophies of God's grace—we find that we can depend on God's grace, His wisdom, and His own faithfulness to us. And we find comfort knowing that the Lord truly has more than enough of His marvelous grace for each of us.

CHAPTER 6

PERFECTLY SANE

EVERY SO OFTEN, I read a verse in the Bible that is a real attention-getter—one that causes me to pause in contemplation or that, perhaps, sparks my imagination. Here is one of those verses:

> *A crowd soon gathered around Jesus, and they saw the man who had been possessed by the legion of demons. He was sitting there fully clothed and perfectly sane, and they were all afraid.* (Mark 5:15)

If I read only this verse, and didn't know the story behind it, I would have to pause to ask some questions. "So the man is sitting there with clothes on and is in his right mind. Why is that significant enough to mention? And why are the other people afraid of him?"

Of course, the answers to these questions and more are revealed in the rest of the story. When I read the entire story of the fully-clothed and perfectly-sane man in the Bible, it plays out in my mind like an intriguing movie.

❦ ❦

Jesus had been ministering on the western shore of the Sea of Galilee when He told His disciples He wanted to cross over to the other side of the lake. It was on this trip across the lake when they experienced the huge tempest that threatened to sink their boat—when Jesus calmed the storm.[28]

Continuing their trip across the lake on calmer water, they arrived on the eastern shore of the Sea of Galilee in the region of the Gerasenes.[29] And it was there where Jesus and His disciples met the man who was possessed with a legion of demons.

> *So they arrived at the other side of the lake, in the region of the Gerasenes. When Jesus climbed out of the boat, a man possessed by an evil spirit came out from the tombs to meet him.*
>
> *This man lived in the burial caves and could no longer be restrained, even with a chain. Whenever he was put into chains and shackles—as he often was—he snapped the chains from his wrists and smashed the shackles. No one was strong enough to subdue him. Day and night he wandered among the burial caves and in the hills, howling and cutting himself with sharp stones.*
>
> (Mark 5:1-5)

The man Jesus met after getting out of the boat was anything but sane. No doubt all the people in that area knew the man who lived among the tombs as someone who was literally out of his mind. Considering his

---

28 Luke 8:22-25.

29 In the gospels of Mark and Luke, the area is called the "region of the Gerasenes" (Mark 5:1; Luke 8:26). Matthew calls the area the "region of the Gadarenes" (Matthew 8:28). It is commonly held that the event took place on the shore of the lake just outside the town of Gergesa—modern Kursi—which is the only place on the eastern shore that has a steep hillside overlooking the lake as described in Mark 5:13.

violent behavior and unusual strength—which, it seems, was only the result of the demonic influence within him—I'm sure the people did their best to avoid him.

When Jesus arrived on the scene, He encountered a man bound by mental and spiritual darkness brought on by the evil spirit controlling him. Demon-possessed people suffer terribly under the influence of satanic control. When evil spirits take up residence inside people, they distort their thinking and affect their physical actions and responses. No one with right thinking would choose to live among the dead—among the tombs and burial caves—but that's where the man lived. According to Luke's account of the event, "for a long time he had been homeless and naked, living in the tombs outside the town."[30]

When Jesus arrived on the shore and got out of the boat, a naked, unkempt, shell of a human being covered with scars and wounds—some of which may still have been bleeding—ran out of the tombs to meet him.

> *When Jesus was still some distance away, the man saw him, ran to meet him, and bowed low before him. With a shriek, he screamed, "Why are you interfering with me, Jesus, Son of the Most High God? In the name of God, I beg you, don't torture me!" For Jesus had already said to the spirit, "Come out of the man, you evil spirit."*
>
> (Mark 5:6-8)

When reading this in the past, I have wondered if the man's desperation for deliverance played any part in him running to meet Jesus and bowing before Him. But it's unlikely that the man even knew who Jesus was. And if he didn't know Jesus as either teacher or healer, then there was no reason for him to go to Jesus thinking He could deliver him from his pain.

But the demons knew Jesus!

30 Luke 8:27.

The man was under the control of demons. And no demon would willingly or intentionally allow its host to go to Jesus to be freed of its influence. But truly, neither the man nor the demons were in control of that situation. There was something remarkable going on, and it involved a powerful display of both God's authority and grace.

When the man opened his mouth, it wasn't the man's spirit at all who cried out for deliverance. It was an evil spirit who spoke.

A demon was in firm control of that man and his actions. Kneeling before Jesus in forced submission, it was a demon who spoke in a state of panic and pleaded with Jesus not to torture him.

Something was at work that was powerful and, perhaps. unexplainable to people whose minds are not in tune with spiritual matters. But to us, who know something about the war that is raging in the spirit world, it should come as no surprise.

Jesus stepped off the boat with purpose, and the demons knew their time had come to submit themselves to Christ's authority.

☙ ❧

Mark wrote that the man could no longer be restrained. It appears that the people who lived in the town and surrounding countryside had given up on him. They had tried in the past to control him, but all their attempts at doing so had failed, and he was left to wander among the tombs and continue his self-destructive behavior.

He was an outcast from society. No one could help him. And I can imagine that, as long as he stayed in his place, no one saw the need to even try. They lacked the power to do anything about his situation. But there was one very special man who could, and He had just arrived on the scene.

Evil spirits are still active in the world today. And just as the man possessed with the legion of demons needed someone to intervene to bring deliverance and sanity to his miserable existence, there are people today who need the same thing. They need Jesus to step off the boat and into their lives, and that happens today as His followers minister to the needs of people in the power of the Holy Spirit. We are the ones now tasked with physically bringing the message of salvation and deliverance to people living in spiritual bondage.

But how are we to do it?

For starters, we need to understand that followers of Christ indeed confront the forces of evil. We need to realize that, as Christians, our greatest enemies are not people but the evil powers now active in the spirit world. Then, we need to go to our Lord for resources to use against them, put our faith in Christ, and allow Him to prepare us to stand firm in the battle.

In his New Testament letter to the Ephesian believers, the apostle Paul addressed Satan's evil strategies and how believers can overcome them.

> *A final word: Be strong in the Lord and in his mighty power. Put on all of God's armor so that you will be able to stand firm against all strategies of the devil. For we are not fighting against flesh-and-blood enemies, but against evil rulers and authorities of the unseen world, against mighty powers in this dark world, and against evil spirits in the heavenly places.*
>
> *Therefore, put on every piece of God's armor so you will be able to resist the enemy in the time of evil. Then after the battle you will still be standing firm.*
>
> *Stand your ground, putting on the belt of truth and the body armor of God's righteousness. For shoes, put on the peace that comes from the Good News so that you will be fully prepared. In addition to all of these, hold up the shield of faith to stop the fiery arrows of the devil. Put on salvation as your helmet, and take the sword of the Spirit, which is the word of God.*
>
> *Pray in the Spirit at all times and on every occasion. Stay alert and be persistent in your prayers for all believers everywhere.* (Ephesians 6:10-18)

If we are going to meet the challenges before us, we must be in a right relationship with God and spend time praying and reading God's Word so that we are fully equipped to stand firm in spiritual battle. We are no match for Satan in our own strength.[31] We must be fully reliant upon God and walk in His power. And to every vestige of spiritual darkness, we must speak the name of Jesus Christ, who is indeed our victory.

☙ ❧

As the man knelt before Jesus on the shore of the Sea of Galilee, while the demon spoke through the man to plead for mercy, Jesus did not hesitate to react with authority.

> *Then Jesus demanded, "What is your name?"*
>
> *And he replied, "My name is Legion, because there are many of us inside this man." Then the evil spirits begged him again and again not to send them to some distant place. There happened to be a large herd of pigs feeding on the hillside nearby. "Send us into those pigs," the spirits begged. "Let us enter them."*
>
> *So Jesus gave them permission. The evil spirits came out of the man and entered the pigs, and the entire herd of about 2,000 pigs plunged down the steep hillside into the lake and drowned in the water.* (Mark 5:9-13)

One encounter with Jesus freed that man from bondage. In one moment, the man was possessed by many demons; in the very next moment, he was totally free of them.

It's worth noting at this point the context between what we just read in the thirteenth verse and what we read of the people's responses

31 Witness the account of the seven sons of Sceva in Acts 19:13-16.

beginning with verse fourteen, quoted below. Think about this before we go on:

A legion can be understood as referring to the number of men in a large Roman army division. It is strictly a Roman term, and it was used by the demon in a territory ruled by Rome. A Roman legion consisted of between 3,000 and 6,000 soldiers.

The demon said his name was "Legion, because there are many of us inside this man." With the number of soldiers in a legion in mind, one can see how an entire herd of around 2,000 pigs could be so tormented that they plunged down the steep hillside into the lake. There were more than enough demons in that poor man to infest the entire herd of pigs.

> *The herdsmen fled to the nearby town and the surrounding countryside, spreading the news as they ran. People rushed out to see what had happened.*
>
> *A crowd soon gathered around Jesus, and they saw the man who had been possessed by the legion of demons. He was sitting there fully clothed and perfectly sane, and they were all afraid.* (Mark 5:14-15)

Two thousand pigs make a huge herd of swine, and in those days, there were no fences to confine them. Such a large herd required a correspondingly large number of herdsmen to care for them. Imagine all those herdsmen fanning out over the town and countryside, frantically telling people about what happened.

People soon came from all directions to where Jesus was with His disciples. As the people gathered around them, there was the man, sitting down talking with them. His emotions had calmed. His mind had cleared. He was carrying on a perfectly sane and logical conversation with Jesus and His followers.

The man was no longer howling and running around. He was no longer trying to injure himself in any way. He was fully clothed. To those gathered there, the man looked and acted perfectly normal.

The citizens of that country knew about the man, and they were shocked and amazed. But they were NOT thrilled with the results of Jesus' ministry. In fact, they were all afraid.

From our perspective, as Christians, we would expect the crowds to be overjoyed that the bound man was finally free. But Jesus' actions were not well-received by the herdsmen and many people in the crowd.

> *Then those who had seen what happened told the others about the demon-possessed man and the pigs. And the crowd began pleading with Jesus to go away and leave them alone.* (Mark 5:16-17)

The people clearly didn't understand the importance or value of Jesus' exertion of authority and power, and they reacted negatively. It was because of their self-interest that they begged Jesus to go away. Their reaction is similar to so many other instances when Jesus was—and still is—rejected by people.

You see, they were not afraid of the man sitting there—the man whose mind had suddenly been made sane. What they feared was what might happen if Jesus didn't leave.

To those people, the value of a soul being delivered could not rise above the value of the pigs that were lost. The positive work of Jesus negatively affected their economy, and they didn't like it. They were satisfied with the status quo of their lives.[32]

But while the other people wanted Jesus to leave, the man who had been delivered showed gratitude by telling others about the miraculous power of the One who saved him.

> *As Jesus was getting into the boat, the man who had been demon possessed begged to go with him.*

32 If this sounds strange to you, think of how Paul's ministry in Ephesus was so successful that a city-wide riot was instigated against the Christians by the artisans who made a living making and selling silver shrines of the goddess Artemis. Paul's partners in ministry—traveling companions from Macedonia—Gaius and Aristarchus, would likely have been killed if the mayor of Ephesus had not been able to speak reason to the crowd and get it to disperse, Acts 19:23-41.

> *But Jesus said, "No, go home to your family, and tell them everything the Lord has done for you and how merciful he has been."*
>
> *So the man started off to visit the Ten Towns of that region and began to proclaim the great things Jesus had done for him; and everyone was amazed at what he told them.* (Mark 5:18-20)

I suppose the reactions of people today aren't really very different—some express fear or even disdain for the presence of God's power, and others express their sincere gratitude for it. Jesus certainly couldn't satisfy everyone with His ministry, and it's clear that we won't satisfy everyone with ours.

But praise God, the story didn't end with the people's rejection of Jesus. According to the story, the people of the ten towns, who heard the man's testimony, were responsive—amazed—at what he told them. The good news Jesus came to bring was getting out. The man who had previously been in bondage to evil spirits was free to share the wonderful Good News of God's grace, and the people responded.

That man became a walking, talking, living trophy of God's grace. And it was all because Jesus intentionally traveled across the Sea of Galilee to deliver him from a literal legion of demons.

☙ ❧

The people in the ten towns were amazed at the man's testimony. I, too, respond with not only amazement at what God did in his life but also with gratitude for God's power and grace-filled keeping displayed in my own life.

As we experience the ups and downs of life, at times, we find that we have drifted into unclear (and sometimes unreasonable) thinking. I'm discovering that my greatest preemptive strategy—and my most effective restorative strategy—to combat wrong thinking is to daily immerse myself in God's Word.

This story of the demon-possessed man causes me to think of a recent experience I had.

In Chapter One, I told you about the Bridge Ministry. One day, while I was serving the homeless under the Jefferson Street Bridge, I met a young man named Samuel. His two friends introduced Samuel to me, and one of the two friends began telling me about him.

The girl explained to me that Samuel had been a perfectly normal high school student and had always earned good grades in school. Then one day, for some unknown reason, he suddenly lost his ability to think or communicate normally.

In her words, "He lost his mind."

Based on what his friends told me about him, and from what I could observe of him and feel in my spirit, I sensed that he was battling a demonic attack. He had somehow opened himself up to evil influences. Even if he was not demon-possessed, he was surely being severely oppressed by the enemy to the point that it was destroying his life.

I looked into Samuel's eyes, and I sensed a desperate longing in him to be restored to right thinking. I laid my hands on his head and began to pray for him in the healing name of Jesus. After praying, I could see that hope began to shine forth from his eyes. I could tell that he was able to focus his mind and connect with me.

I handed him a Bible and instructed him to either read from the New Testament or have it read to him daily. Led by the prompting of the Holy Spirit, I assured him that, if he would indeed read the Scriptures daily, within one year, his mind would be restored.

I don't know what events contributed to Samuel's condition. And I have yet to find out if Samuel has followed my admonition. I don't know what his condition is today. But I do know one thing without question: The healing power of Jesus Christ can bring deliverance and restoration to a confused and oppressed mind.

I have confidence in what the Holy Spirit had me tell Samuel. I know that, if he does what I told him to do, the Lord will bring restoration to both his heart and mind. The Word of God never fails. It never returns void.[33] I know Samuel's right thinking can be restored as the Word of God is placed within his heart.

☙ ❧

Praise God that Jesus took on human form and walked among mankind as He purposefully demonstrated His authority over every ungodly influence. Demonic activity and confusion must retreat at Jesus' command! [34] And the authority to do the same work He did is ours today, as we pattern our lives after Christ and submit to the leadership of His Holy Spirit.[35]

In the story of the man living among the tombs, the man's encounter with Jesus brought to him right thinking. Because of the man's encounter with the Living Word, he was changed from being a raving lunatic to being perfectly sane.

That man's restoration motivated him to share the news of how God can take a person who doesn't have the ability to think and act in a reasonable and logical way and turn his life around. Just as that man shared what God did for him, I am eager to share what the Lord has done for me—to share how merciful God has been in helping me think straight.

God actively seeks out and extends His grace to those who have troubled minds and needy hearts. I'm grateful He did that in such a marvelous way for the man who lived among the tombs. If Jesus had not done all that He did, the man's life would have been doomed to a sad ending, and others would not have heard about Jesus.

If your mind needs to be renovated and renewed, remember the man whom Jesus delivered from the legion of demons—the man who was once considered a lost cause, but whom Jesus made perfectly sane. Like that man, as our hearts and minds are healed and restored, we too become the trophies of God's incredible grace.

---

33 "So shall my word be that goeth forth out of my mouth: it shall not return unto me void, but it shall accomplish that which I please, and it shall prosper in the thing whereto I sent it" (Isaiah 55:11 KJV).

"It is the same with my word. I send it out, and it always produces fruit. It will accomplish all I want it to, and it will prosper everywhere I send it" (Isaiah 55:11 NLT).

34 Mark 1:21-28; Matthew 12:22-29; Luke 4:14-19.

35 "I tell you the truth, anyone who believes in me will do the same works I have done, and even greater works, because I am going to be with the Father. You can ask for anything in my name, and I will do it, so that the Son can bring glory to the Father. Yes, ask me for anything in my name, and I will do it!" (John 14:12-14).

CHAPTER 7

MOVED WITH COMPASSION

ON MOST DAYS, it seems our lives are filled with lists, tasks, and daily routines. We wake up, get ready for work, take the kids to school, pick them up, eat dinner, go to bed, and do it all over again the next day. Although there is certainly great benefit in fulfilling the regular duties of our own lives, we experience a different kind of fulfillment when we pause to compassionately touch the life of someone else.

Our attention is usually arrested when we observe or read about someone performing a special act of kindness. We both notice and greatly admire fellow humans who deliberately choose to act with compassion. Heartfelt compassion toward fellow humans seems increasingly rare, so when we witness an act of kindness birthed from deep compassion, we tend to be emotionally moved—affected by an obvious display of selflessness.

Because of our sin nature, left to our own devices, we tend to focus more on ourselves than others. Even in our present-day culture of heightened connectedness through technology, we persist in interacting with others on a surface level—with a sense of detached concern. And we are surprised when people do otherwise.

Although people may think their detached concern for others serves a good purpose, it's through our care for others that we learn the true value of becoming less focused on ourselves. Several years ago, I remember hearing about an unexpected act of kindness—a gesture of compassion woven within the story of Santa Claus.

The concept of Santa Claus came from a real person named Saint Nicholas. He has been remembered and made famous by his gifts of compassion—the origin of our tradition of gift-giving at Christmastime. Saint Nicholas was a devout Christian man who served as a bishop during the fourth century in Myra, an area in present-day Turkey. While he was a young man, both of his parents died, leaving him a substantial monetary inheritance. Rather than simply using his inheritance for himself, he chose to help the poor and infirm.

There are many legends surrounding the life of Saint Nicholas. One story reports that he saved three men who were falsely imprisoned and sentenced to death. Another story is told of his compassionate act toward a father and his three daughters. The poor father could not provide dowries to allow his daughters to marry, so he considered selling his daughters into servitude.

After hearing about that family's desperate situation, Nicholas secretly went to their house at night and left a bag of money. He did that three separate times—once for each daughter. On Nicholas' third visit, the father realized who had bestowed the acts of kindness on his family and thanked Nicholas for his compassionate generosity.[36] The father, in his poverty, could never repay Nicholas for such a generous act of compassion.

Many people attribute Saint Nicholas' example of generosity to his determination to follow Christ's example in giving His life for all

36 "Saint Nicholas Biography." *Biography.com*. Published 12/7/2017, updated 12/12/19. https://www.biography.com/people/st-nicholas-204635.

humanity. What gracious kindness God bestowed upon us through the gift of His Son! If this was indeed Saint Nicholas' motivation for his own giving, it's not hard to imagine why he was so compassionately generous. Christ's sacrificial gift is truly the greatest model of compassionate giving for us to follow.

☙ ❧

Compassion is defined by the Merriam-Webster Dictionary as "sympathetic consciousness of others' distress together with a desire to alleviate it."[37] When we allow our hearts to be moved with deep compassion, we are prompted to act to bring change to a person's situation.

There is a Greek word used in the New Testament that describes this kind of deep compassion. The word, *splagchnizomai*, means "to be moved as to one's bowels, hence to be moved with compassion, have compassion (for the bowels were thought to be the seat of love and pity)."[38]

Splagchnizomai doesn't describe an ordinary sense of compassion—one that only looks on another's situation with pity. This word describes compassion that is gut-wrenching and that causes one to be moved to action. In the New Testament, *splagchnizomai* is only used of Jesus and by Jesus as He tells the stories of the good Samaritan[39] and the father of the prodigal son.[40]

In the parables of the good Samaritan and the father of the prodigal son, both men are described by Jesus as moved with compassion to love and act beyond what might be considered normal human behavior.

The good Samaritan showed great compassion in using his own money to tend to the needs of a bloody, beaten, Jewish traveler. The Jews showed great disdain for the Samaritans, yet that Samaritan man took care of the Jewish man's needs.

---

37 "Compassion." Merriam-Webster.com Dictionary, Merriam-Webster, https://www.merriam-webster.com/dictionary/compassion.

38 Thayer and Smith. "Greek Lexicon entry for Splagchnizomai." *The NAS New Testament Greek Lexicon.* 1999. https://www.biblestudytools.com/lexicons/greek/nas/splagchnizomai.html.

39 Luke 10:30-37.

40 Luke 15:11-32.

The father in the story of the prodigal son had every right to turn away his ungrateful son when he attempted to return. Instead, he drew him in and celebrated his return home. To show such kindness—such compassion—is unusual. And God showed unusual compassion toward us in giving to us the gift of His Son Jesus.

It amazes me that God would show us such kindness.

That God would draw near enough to His creation to understand our pain, and be compelled to intervene, is really an amazing thought. Throughout world history, even false gods thought to hold great power were not attributed such compassion. But our God stepped down from heaven to walk among His creation, understand our frailty, and grace us with His compassionate care.

☙ ❧

There are numerous examples of Jesus' acts of compassion throughout the New Testament, but I want to focus on one story in particular recorded by Luke—a story of a widow whose only son had died. Jesus' compassion for the woman moved Him to act on her behalf.

Jesus' encounter with that woman took place early in His ministry. Great crowds of people had begun to follow Jesus. Some probably followed Him out of curiosity, while others perhaps followed Him out of respect for His words of wisdom and authority over sickness and disease. As Jesus, His disciples, and the crowd following Him approached the widow's hometown of Nain, they came face to face with a large funeral procession.

> *As he drew near to the gate of the town, behold, a man who had died was being carried out, the only son of his mother, and she was a widow, and a considerable crowd from the town was with her.*
>
> *And when the Lord saw her, he had compassion on her and said to her, "Do not weep." Then he came up and*

> *touched the bier, and the bearers stood still. And he said, "Young man, I say to you, arise."* (Luke 7:12-14, ESV)

Jesus stepped into the woman's desperate situation and met her most immediate need—the restoration of the life of her only son. No one asked Jesus to perform a miracle that day, but Jesus raised the young man back to life in an act of His compassionate grace. How beautiful it is that Jesus, the Son of God, would be so moved by the distress of His creation that He would feel *splagchnizomai.*

Although the story focuses on the raising of the woman's son, Luke specifically states that "she was a widow." This is a critical piece of information in the story because, as a widow, the woman had no other means of support except her only son. Without him, she was at great risk of living a life of poverty.

In Biblical times, when a woman's husband died and was no longer there to support her, she became reliant on her living son(s) for her survival. God shows great concern for the livelihoods of widows throughout Scripture.

> *Father to the fatherless, defender of widows—this is God, whose dwelling is holy.* (Psalm 68:5)

> *Pure and genuine religion in the sight of God the Father means caring for orphans and widows in their distress and refusing to let the world corrupt you.* (James 1:27)

> *Take care of any widow who has no one else to care for her.* (1 Timothy 5:3)

Compassion from the heart of God reminds us that we are cared for even in times of deepest difficulty. The widow from Nain in Luke's story can remind us of our own vulnerability, as the changes in life produced by loss can certainly be frightening. We start to ask "what if" questions when we're feeling vulnerable: "What if my healing never comes?" "What if we lose our financial footing?" "What if that relationship is never restored?" We worry about the what ifs because we can't see how God's hand will protect and steady us amid what we think might or might not happen.

We as humans have a tendency to project our fear onto the future in times of difficulty and loss. My mother had a saying that she quite often reminded me of:

> Today's grace is sufficient for today, but don't try to project today's grace onto tomorrow's problems. The grace for tomorrow will be there when you get there.

God's intervening grace in our lives is always on time! He is present with us today, and He will be compassionately present with us in each of our tomorrows—no matter what comes.

I imagine the widow of Nain had mentally assessed her own situation after her son's death and couldn't have guessed how God would intervene on her behalf. And yet He did. God in the flesh showed up to change her future. As the widow, along with the crowd accompanying her, reached the town's gate, Jesus was there, present with compassion, ready to grant grace-filled hope to the widow for her tomorrow.

Jesus' compassion was evident for all to see as He spoke to her, touched the bier, and called the young man to arise. It is significant that Jesus "touched the bier, and the bearers stood still." In the Jewish tradition of burial, the linen-wrapped corpse was placed on an open bier as opposed to a closed coffin. The body of the young man lay on the open bier for all to see.

The Levitical laws of the time considered Jesus' act of touching the bier unclean.[41] That act certainly would have caused those carrying the bier to stop and stand still. Jesus, a respected Teacher, knew that touching the bier would arrest the attention of all who were present. But the enemies of Christ would not be able to criticize Jesus with any authority for being unclean if the young man was raised from the dead! In that moment, those present witnessed Christ's power over death as

41 Numbers 19:11.

the young man sat up and spoke. The people responded by glorifying God and spreading the report far and wide about Jesus' powerful act.

> *And the dead man sat up and began to speak, and Jesus gave him to his mother. Fear seized them all, and they glorified God, saying, "A great prophet has arisen among us!" and "God has visited his people!" And this report about him spread through the whole of Judea and all the surrounding country.* (Luke 7:15-17, ESV)

That day, the people of Nain experienced the presence and power of Jesus Christ as He was moved with compassion to intervene in the lives of the widow, her son, and everyone present.

As we consider the events of our own lives, we surely must admit that we have seen God's gracious intervention again and again. Just as the young man began to speak when Jesus' words restored his life, and just as the crowd spoke of Jesus' greatness, we too must be willing to recount God's acts of restorative grace in our lives. Every restorative touch of God in our lives speaks of His compassion toward us.

God's grace is made evident through His compassionate acts toward us. That is the very nature of the gospel message. People are drawn to the gospel as we speak of its power and beauty. We become conduits of His grace as we act compassionately toward others.

This past weekend, I had the privilege of becoming a conduit of compassionate grace (along with the rest of my church family). My home church, Cornerstone Nashville, provided Christmas gifts to several terminally ill children and their families. Through a large offering taken weeks beforehand, we were able to bless the families with an abundance of gifts, making many of those children's wishes come true.

One young cancer patient wanted his siblings to be able to go to the zoo. The family had recently come from Thailand, and a trip to the zoo was beyond their financial means. Our church family gave them year-long passes to the zoo. Another family had always dreamed of taking a family vacation to Disney World, but the treatments for their child's sickness had consumed all their resources. We arranged for an all-expense-paid trip for them. A seventeen-year-old leukemia patient had a dream of driving a high-end sports car on a closed track. He'll be taking that drive soon at a motor speedway in Atlanta.

The monetary offerings provided the means by which we made those dreams come true, but compassion is what initiated the process. We were moved with compassion to action on their behalf. As we bestowed gifts upon those families, we also prayed for them—for God's peace to surround them and for God's grace to heal them. By carrying out those compassionate acts, we were able to demonstrate the beauty of the gospel of Jesus Christ. That's grace at work through the compassionate acts of God's children!

ꕥ

As shown to us in the story of the widow of Nain, Jesus demonstrated and illustrated for us what his compassion looks like. We must come to understand, receive, and impart that compassion to others as Christ's representatives in our world.

How beautiful that both the widow and her son stand as trophies of God's marvelous grace! Both of their lives testify to God's care and compassion. They were given a hopeful future on earth when none seemed to exist for them. As we read their story, we are inspired by it to lay hold of the hope and future God has for us today—and for others, as His compassion leads us into ministry. But not only are the widow of Nain and her son trophies of grace; so is Christ.

As we emulate His acts of grace, proclaim them, and demonstrate them to others in need, we can expect His grace to continue to work in powerful and amazing ways. We can expect many more people around us to become trophies of God's grace.

CHAPTER 8

RESCUED AND SET FREE

WHEN I WAS a child, I learned many valuable lessons from my parents and other family members. As a child, I learned by example. That's common. But even as adults, we learn from the examples people set before us—both good and bad. Society teaches us social norms (which can be good, but which often conflict with our own moral convictions). Friendships and acquaintances grant us opportunities to learn from both joyful interactions and painful experiences.

Many of the lessons we learn are beneficial to our development as Christians, but some are not. Some are negative lessons. When we observe other people living their daily lives around us, we sometimes see evidence of the negative lessons they've learned. Instead of exhibiting kindness and generosity, some people exhibit opposite traits, learned from individuals who exemplified negative characteristics.

We see blatant acts of selfishness and wonder why those individuals weren't taught to consider others' well-being in their decisions. Or perhaps negativity has completely obscured their perspective of joy-filled living, and we wonder why they didn't emerge from their growing-up years with a more balanced outlook on life.

Many people grew up learning selfish, uncaring behavior from those who experienced the same upbringing. As the saying goes, we tend to reproduce who we are. Others, of course, are simply copying or responding to negative behavior they have seen in others, regardless of how they themselves were raised. But for sure, the tendency to exhibit negative behavior often accompanies those who are bound in harmful thought processes and unhealthy relationships.

Reproducing who we are is a sobering reality of living life with others. Intentionally or unintentionally, we influence those around us. We are wise to ask ourselves this question: "Am I, through my example, influencing others to be bound in unhealthy behaviors, or am I encouraging them to be free to interact in healthy ways?"

The realization that I am influencing others—my own children included—by my example leaves me utterly dependent on the grace of God. That thought often drives me to my knees in prayer. As my children were growing up, they tended to exemplify my attitudes, preferences, and perspectives. We spent our days together, so my influence on them was unmistakable—sometimes unmistakably positive, and sometimes unmistakably negative.

Much to my delight, they would often display maturity and unselfish behavior. But if the words that came out of their mouths and the behaviors they displayed were undesirable, they made me realize I needed to check my words and behaviors. It was often I who needed to change.

In many ways, they were simply copying my example. It was God's grace that both allowed me to see my need for change and helped me to bring about that change.

☙ ❧

When I think about the need to change—the need to find freedom from unhealthy ways of thinking and unhealthy actions—my mind drifts to Saul (also referred to as Paul, the Greek version of his name, the author of much of the New Testament). Having received the best

Jewish education by the most revered teachers, Saul reflected through his thinking—and his behavior—the religious training given to him.

Often called a Pharisee among Pharisees,[42] Saul zealously defended the religious system and set about destroying those who threatened to discredit the beliefs on which he had based his behaviors and ways of thinking.[43] Saul was sincere in defending the Jewish way of life—the Law of Moses and the religious traditions of his heritage. His sincerity drove him to protect the Law at any cost—and that cost became the livelihood, and in some cases the very lives, of those who had chosen to follow the teachings of Christ.[44]

Saul, like many of his Jewish contemporaries, had great difficulty reconciling the prophetic expectation of the Messiah with the coming of Jesus. Jewish history and prophetic teachings recorded in the Old Testament spoke of the coming Messiah. His work was prophesied to be far-reaching; but by that time in history, many Jews were merely anticipating a Savior who would rescue them from their Roman oppressors. So when Messiah came as an itinerant teacher in humility rather than a conquering king, many religiously devout Jews didn't recognize Him.

Saul was one of those religiously devout Jews. He sincerely defended the faith he had been taught and believed. His sincerity drove him to destroy the people who accepted Jesus as the true Messiah. But in a life-changing moment of grace, God intervened in Saul's destructive rampage of arresting and imprisoning followers of Christ.

Saul encountered the Messiah, Jesus Christ, on the road to Damascus.

> *As he was approaching Damascus on this mission, a light from heaven suddenly shone down around him. He fell to the ground and heard a voice saying to him, "Saul! Saul! Why are you persecuting me?"*

---

42 "I was circumcised when I was eight days old. I am a pure-blooded citizen of Israel and a member of the tribe of Benjamin—a real Hebrew if there ever was one! I was a member of the Pharisees, who demand the strictest obedience to the Jewish law" (Philippians 3:5).

43 "You know what I was like when I followed the Jewish religion—how I violently persecuted God's church. I did my best to destroy it. I was far ahead of my fellow Jews in my zeal for the traditions of my ancestors" (Galatians 1:13-14).

44 "But Saul was going everywhere to destroy the church. He went from house to house, dragging out both men and women to throw them into prison" (Acts 8:3).

"Who are you, lord?" Saul asked.

And the voice replied, "I am Jesus, the one you are persecuting! Now get up and go into the city, and you will be told what you must do."

The men with Saul stood speechless, for they heard the sound of someone's voice but saw no one! Saul picked himself up off the ground, but when he opened his eyes he was blind. So his companions led him by the hand to Damascus. He remained there blind for three days and did not eat or drink.

Now there was a believer in Damascus named Ananias. The Lord spoke to him in a vision, calling, "Ananias!"

"Yes, Lord!" he replied.

The Lord said, "Go over to Straight Street, to the house of Judas. When you get there, ask for a man from Tarsus named Saul. He is praying to me right now. I have shown him a vision of a man named Ananias coming in and laying hands on him so he can see again."

"But Lord," exclaimed Ananias, "I've heard many people talk about the terrible things this man has done to the believers in Jerusalem! And he is authorized by the leading priests to arrest everyone who calls upon your name."

But the Lord said, "Go, for Saul is my chosen instrument to take my message to the Gentiles and to kings, as well as to the people of Israel. And I will show him how much he must suffer for my name's sake."

> *So Ananias went and found Saul. He laid his hands on him and said, "Brother Saul, the Lord Jesus, who appeared to you on the road, has sent me so that you might regain your sight and be filled with the Holy Spirit." Instantly something like scales fell from Saul's eyes, and he regained his sight. Then he got up and was baptized.*
>
> (Acts 9:3-18)

Saul had been convinced that he was defending the right religious system. It took a direct encounter with Jesus to correct his thinking. Saul had become a prisoner to his misguided perspective. But his life-changing encounter set him free to pursue Jesus Christ and the new covenant made possible by His sacrifice on the cross.

☙ ❧

Our perspective can fall prey more often than we realize to a narrowed, misguided thought pattern. Simply participating in this world's system and being exposed to the evil around us can negatively influence our perspectives. As we go about our days, our thoughts can easily align with worldly thinking rather than biblical thinking. When we don't immerse ourselves in the Word of God, our minds can get off track. We sometimes need to be rescued from our own erroneous thought patterns and misguided perspectives.

I'm so grateful the standard of right-thinking—the Word of God—is available to us. Romans chapter 12 contains one of my favorite New Testament verses. It's a favorite because the verse reminds me how to regain (or gain for the first time) correct perspectives. And how beautifully appropriate it is that Paul—who had been steeped in misguided thinking—wrote these words:

> *Don't copy the behavior and customs of this world, but let God transform you into a new person by changing the*

> *way you think. Then you will learn to know God's will for you, which is good and pleasing and perfect.*
> (Romans 12:2)

Paul was speaking from first-hand experience. When Paul met Jesus on the road to Damascus, he submitted himself to the lordship of Christ, and God brought about a much-needed change in Paul's thinking. Because of that, Paul changed his direction. He moved from working against God's purposes to cooperating with them. Then, with a renewed mind and godly actions, Paul was able to lead others by his example to do the same.

The evidence of Paul's transformation was made clear—the very people who earlier had been fearful of Saul's destructive acts were praising God because of the change in his life.

> *All they knew was that people were saying, "The one who used to persecute us is now preaching the very faith he tried to destroy." And they praised God because of me.*
> (Galatians 1:23-24)

There is something incredibly powerful about the testimony of a transformed life. Significant change is sometimes hard for us to achieve. We tend to avoid it. We tend to cling to comfort and familiarity as default responses, and to push away the idea of making significant changes. It's easier not to change our current ways of doing things—ultimately, our ways of thinking. But if we want to see significant change in our lives, it begins with changing the way we think.

People who learn the positive lessons God teaches—people who respond to the Word and the voice of God and engage in the difficult effort of changing the way they think—are those who are able to move past discomfort to make significant changes in their lives. Paul was one of those people, and his life now stands as a powerful testimony of God's grace.

❧ ❧

In my growing-up years, I was a competitive gymnast. I truly loved gymnastics and spent as many hours a week as I could at the gym, learning new skills and practicing for upcoming competitions. When I wasn't in school or at church, I was in the gym. Even when the gym was closed, I was practicing my routines in the backyard of our southern California home.

One day, my dad surprised me with a balance beam that he had specially made for me so I could practice my beam routines in our backyard. I spent many hours perfecting my routines on that balance beam. Gymnastics became my life—my reason for waking up in the morning, and my passionate pursuit each day.

Overall, participating in gymnastics was a tremendously good experience in my life, but there was a brief period of time when I allowed it to become an unhealthy obsession. During that time, I allowed gymnastics to negatively consume my thoughts and actions. Everything I did was focused on the purpose of becoming a better gymnast.

I began to choose my food carefully, weighing out in my mind which foods would perfect my body's ability to perform. I looked at myself in the mirror for the purpose of honing my physical body for efficiency and effectiveness in winning competitions. And before long, I fell prey to the cycle of anorexia nervosa.

Anorexia nervosa, as described by the Mayo Clinic, is "an eating disorder characterized by an abnormally low body weight, an intense fear of gaining weight, and a distorted perception of weight. People with anorexia place a high value on controlling their weight and shape, using extreme efforts that tend to significantly interfere with their lives."[45]

When I looked at myself in the mirror, I saw an overweight young gymnast. I would step on the scale and plan how I could make the numbers go down by the next day. I was practicing in the gym more and more hours each week, and I was eating less and less food. I couldn't see what I was doing to myself. The image I saw in the mirror day after

45 "Anorexia nervosa." *Mayoclinic.org.* https://www.mayoclinic.org/diseases-conditions/anorexia-nervosa/symptoms-causes/syc-20353591.

day never changed, although the descending numbers on the scale were rewarding my efforts in limiting my eating.

Finally, after several weeks of this anorexic cycle, my mother said to me, "Debbie, if you don't stop losing weight, I'll have to take you out of gymnastics."

By speaking those words, my mother became my enemy. In my distorted thinking, I convinced myself that she simply wanted to prevent me from reaching my potential. I still couldn't see myself properly in the mirror, so her threat seemed completely unfounded.

Then, one day, as I rounded the corner into my mother's bedroom with its long, mirrored closets, I caught a glimpse of myself in the mirror. And for the first time in two months, I saw my body as it really was—an unhealthy, skeletal-like frame. The sight of my body in the mirror horrified me.

As I stood there, frightened by what I saw, my eyes observed my image in the mirror shift back to the overweight body I had been seeing all along. At that moment, I realized my mind had deceived me into believing a lie. I knew I needed help. My mother had been right all along. I ran to her and told her what I had seen in the mirror; in time, my mother led me back into healthy living.

Mom told me later that she and my doctor had decided to admit me to the local hospital if a significant change did not take place almost immediately. They prayed together and asked God to open my eyes. They received the answer to their prayers that day, when I momentarily saw myself correctly in the mirror.

Although my physical body healed, and my visual perception eventually was corrected, I had to walk through the transformation of allowing God to heal my self-image. Time spent in His Word helped me learn to see myself the way He sees me—a beautiful, accepted daughter of the One who loves me perfectly.

That experience with anorexia taught me that right thinking is truly found in the Word of God—in His ways of thinking. Through the prayers of my mother and the doctor, and through the Word of God, I was set free to see myself the way God sees me. I was set free from my destructive, downward spiral with anorexia. I was rescued from my thoughts.

God certainly extended His grace to me as He restored my right thinking.

☙ ❧

I rejoice as I think back on God's healing of my mind and my physical body. And I believe my experience allows me to have some insight into what Jesus did when He changed Paul's thinking. Paul's mind was also rescued and set free from his destructive thought patterns.

I can imagine that the apostle Paul rejoiced as God brought him into right thinking and restored his eyesight. The Word himself, Jesus Christ, aligned Paul's thinking with His purposes. And Paul accepted the realignment. That becomes perfectly clear in Paul's writing.

The rest of Paul's life took an entirely new direction. His mind was changed, and his life proved it. Paul's mind was rescued and set free from wrong thinking. He became a right-thinker, and Paul chose to pursue the One who had brought an end to his rampage against the Christ-followers.

Following his encounter with Christ on the Damascus road, Paul immediately ceased his persecution of Christians. Then he moved to Arabia—far away from his hometown. It was only years later that he went to Jerusalem to link arms with the Church in ministry.[46]

In those intervening years, Paul no doubt spent his time getting to know Christ better and gaining insight into what God wanted him to do next.[47] Paul chose to exchange his own comfort and the admiration he had gained among his peers for the privilege of pursuing Christ and allowing Him to continue to transform his thinking. The effect of God's grace in Paul's life has impacted every generation since.

We, too, can find hope in knowing the change that takes place in us can powerfully affect the lives of others. As Christians, changes in our

46 Galatians 1:15-20a

47 "I received my message from no human source, and no one taught me. Instead, I received it by direct revelation from Jesus Christ" (Galatians 1:12).

thinking produced by the Word of God bring much glory to the One who rescues us from our own destructive thinking and sets us free to think and live rightly.

> *He will give eternal life to those who keep on doing good, seeking after the glory and honor and immortality that God offers.* (Romans 2:7)

As we allow His Word to transform our thinking, adjust our perspectives, and influence our actions, we are rescued and set free to think and live according to His Word—His ways. His grace has rescued us, and His Word continues to transform our minds.

Paul's transformed life certainly stands as a trophy before the world. But as I think about how God also rescued me—reached out to me, transformed my mind, and set me free to live in victory—I believe I, too, stand as a trophy of God's incredible grace.

CHAPTER 9

LIFE HAPPENS

I RECENTLY READ a wise adage: "Life is what happens to us while we're busy making other plans." I readily admit that is true.

My mother's recent death reminded me that we are often forced to make adjustments to even our best-laid plans. We buried my mother's body on November 14, 2018. Although she had bravely battled cancer for three years prior to her death, none of us expected her death to come so suddenly.

Her last CT scan revealed that the cancer had spread uncontrollably, and the experimental treatment study in which she was enrolled was deemed no longer effective. She was dismissed from further treatment and encouraged to seek hospice care to offer her physical comfort until her death. On November 1, 2018, my dad and I assisted Mom in all of her hospice-care decisions.

The necessary paperwork was signed, and the first nurse's visits were scheduled. Mom took her last breath only ten days after the hospice intake appointment. Three days after that, we stood at her graveside, where my sister and I read Mom's favorite Scripture and prayed for God to comfort us all.

Life was happening to us—or perhaps it's better said that death was happening to us—while we were planning for a much longer period of time to say goodbye. Looking back on the events, I'm truly grateful for the shortened period of potential suffering for my mom. None of us were prepared for such a short ending to the story of my mom's life, but God was incredibly gracious.

We tend to make our life plans according to what we think should happen next, or with regard to what will make us happy, but we often neglect to see that some of the most impactful moments in life can be found in the disruptions of those plans.

Just when we feel we have our lives under control, an unexpected event reminds us that life doesn't always go the way we think it will. Those unexpected events can often cause us to feel as if we've experienced a death of sorts—the death of our own plans.

We may be experiencing the physical death of a loved one or a friend, or maybe we're experiencing the death of an expected outcome. Maybe the careers we thought would succeed have failed, or the funding for our plans that we were relying on never came through. Perhaps we're walking through the loss of a significant relationship, or maybe we're experiencing the death of a dream.

Each time we experience any kind of significant loss, we're forced to face a new decision: Will we adjust our plans to fit our changing circumstances, or languish in the sorrow of loss?

Admittedly, it takes courage to adjust our thought processes and plans in light of our new realities. It's hard for us to see how unwanted disruptions can produce anything good. After all, we'd no doubt prefer to successfully live out each step of our carefully-planned lives, just as we had imagined them playing out.

But let's be honest; we would likely succumb to the sin of pride if our own plans ruled our lives. James, an apostle of Christ, reminds us that our plans are truly not our own; they belong to Christ.

> *Look here, you who say, "Today or tomorrow we are going to a certain town and will stay there a year. We will do business there and make a profit." How do you know what your life will be like tomorrow? Your life is like the morning fog—it's here a little while, then it's gone. What you ought to say is, "If the Lord wants us to, we will live and do this or that." Otherwise you are boasting about your own pretentious plans, and all such boasting is evil.* (James 4:13-16)

When we recognize that God is the author of our lives and cease to depend on our own plans, we operate in less pride and more humility. Unwanted disruptions in life can create opportunities for us to move toward greater dependence on God, and that will protect our hearts from pride.

God often uses the upsetting of our plans to help us become more dependent on Him. As we learn to lean into the changes of our plans with humble dependence on His leadership, we find a rhythm of life that is both peace-filled and satisfying—even in the face of death.

So then, adverse events that force adjustments to our plans are actually opportunities to experience the grace of God.

❧ ❧

As I contemplate how our adversities lead us to experience God's grace, I'm reminded of the Old Testament story of Daniel.

Daniel lived from about 620 B.C. to 538 B.C.. He was born into a family of royal heritage in the land of Judah in the middle of King Josiah's reign. In Judah's history, there had been many kings who were considered evil—unyielding to God's regulations and standards. But King Josiah was considered one of the righteous kings.[48]

Prior to King Josiah's reign, the scrolls containing God's Laws had been lost, and the Temple, where the people were supposed to worship

48 See Daniel chapter 1-6 and 2 Chronicles chapter 34-35.

only God, had become run-down and defiled with idol worship. During King Josiah's reign, though, the sacred scrolls were recovered, and the Temple was cleansed of idolatrous objects and re-dedicated to the worship of God.

King Josiah was convicted by what was read to him from the sacred scrolls, and he went about reinstituting God's Laws. But there was a problem with that reformation. Although the people performed the righteous deeds prescribed by the Law, their hearts remained unchanged. Outward adherence to the Law only masked their unchanged hearts.

After reigning for thirty-one years, King Josiah was killed in a battle against Egypt, and within four years after his death, Judah returned to its evil ways. God sent prophets to warn the people of their idolatry, but they were comfortable in their sin and chose not to align themselves with God's standards.

This was the national atmosphere in which Daniel was raised. He was aware of what God demanded, and he saw the people around him choosing to live according to their own desires and standards. During that time, Daniel would likely have heard the words spoken by the prophet Jeremiah and watched the people rebuff Jeremiah's words.

Judgment was coming.

> *This is what the Lord of Heaven's Armies says: "Cut down the trees for battering rams. Build siege ramps against the walls of Jerusalem. This is the city to be punished, for she is wicked through and through.*
>
> *"She spouts evil like a fountain. Her streets echo with the sounds of violence and destruction. I always see her sickness and sores. Listen to this warning, Jerusalem, or I will turn from you in disgust. Listen, or I will turn you into a heap of ruins, a land where no one lives."*
>
> *This is what the Lord of Heaven's Armies says: "Even the few who remain in Israel will be picked over again, as*

> *when a harvester checks each vine a second time to pick the grapes that were missed."* (Jeremiah 6:6-9)

God would not allow the people's rebellion to go unpunished. So He appointed Babylon to bring His judgment against the people of Judah. Unfortunately, even those who wholeheartedly served God experienced the consequences of national judgment.

At the time King Nebuchadnezzar of Babylon swept into Jerusalem, Daniel was probably about seventeen years old. Nebuchadnezzar made Judah his vassal state. To demonstrate his dominance, he took many of Jerusalem's wisest men and most beautiful women to Babylon as captives. Daniel and his three friends were among that group.

Surely, captivity was not part of Daniel's life plan, yet he was presented with a new reality, and he had to make a choice. Would he adjust his attitude to fit his new circumstances, or would he languish in the loss of his homeland and his way of life?

Daniel wisely chose to listen to the prophet Jeremiah's predictions and settle into the new plans for his people and his future.

> *This entire land will become a desolate wasteland. Israel and her neighboring lands will serve the king of Babylon for seventy years.* (Jeremiah 25:11)

The people of Judah would be away from their beloved homeland for seventy years. However, Daniel determined to remain faithful to God in the land of his captivity. And God granted him great favor with those in authority over him. Through the reigns of at least four foreign kings (Nebuchadnezzar, Belshazzar, Darius, and Cyrus), Daniel maintained a life fully devoted to God. Daniel spent his entire adult life advising his nation's captors with the unusual wisdom that God granted him.

I imagine that Daniel had to process the death of many things when he was taken captive to Babylon—the death of living in his homeland; the death of going to the Temple to worship; the death of corporate religious fasts and feast days; the death of national identity; and perhaps even the physical death of family and friends during the siege of Jerusalem and the relocation to Babylon.

According to historical records, it appears that Daniel never returned to live in his homeland. Daniel upheld his faithful service to his God even in difficult circumstances—even when life happened. God used Daniel's humility to influence people in the land of his captivity. Daniel's life of dedication to God in those circumstances even caused the rulers he served to recognize the sovereignty and power of his God.[49]

ɷ ɷ

None of us is exempt from unexpected or unwanted changes in life. Like Daniel, we must choose to either adapt to the changes—and weather them with humility and dependence on God—or oppose the changes and stubbornly refuse to adjust our plans. It's our choice.

In making our choices, we must realize that stubborn refusal to adjust robs us of opportunities to experience what God has in mind for our new life circumstances. But when we are willing to humbly trust God in the face of an unknown future. He always makes something good out of what we so often consider bad.

> *You have turned my mourning into joyful dancing. You have taken away my clothes of mourning and clothed me with joy, that I might sing praises to you and not be silent. O Lord my God, I will give you thanks forever!*
> (Psalm 30:11-12)

> *And we know that God causes everything to work together for the good of those who love God and are called according to his purpose for them.* (Romans 8:28)

These are God's grace-filled purposes at work in us—even in our pain. We can be joyful and sing praises because He is good—even when

49 Daniel 2:47, 4:37, 5:11-12, 6:25-27; Ezra 1:1-4.

life happens—and He has a wonderful future reserved for those who love Him. Like Daniel's life demonstrated, our humble, faith-filled responses to pain, discomfort, and trouble can be incredibly influential to those around us.

Daniel certainly stands as a trophy of God's incredible grace. We too can stand as trophies of God's grace in the middle of unwanted disruptions. It's not easy to yield our pain of loss to God during the death of our plans. But God will always be faithful to His children in the face of every circumstance, and He can always be trusted to keep His promises. So don't stop living when life as you know it, or expect it to be, is disrupted.

> *Let us hold tightly without wavering to the hope we affirm, for God can be trusted to keep his promise.*
> (Hebrews 10:23)

Hope without wavering when life happens. God has something good in mind for you!

CHAPTER 10

Prepare the Way

SHE'S COMING! MY joyful anticipation of the arrival of my first grandchild is growing stronger each day. I vividly remember the day I found out I was going to be Mimi—the grandmotherly name my children affectionately chose for me. On that day, my parents, my children, and their spouses had gathered at my house to celebrate my birthday—so I thought.

That evening, we ate dinner together and then moved into the family room to play a game. I requested that we play a word game, because my mother had recently experienced a stroke and was attempting to regain her vocabulary and her speech. Mom always loved words.

It seems that we are a family of wordsmiths. We love to read and write, and some of us are authors, teachers, and public speakers. We've always enjoyed learning new words—long words, curious words, and funny words. So each member of the family came to our gathering that night with an interesting word to share.

We started around our family circle allowing each person to enthusiastically proclaim his or her word and its meaning. Some words were funny, and some were quite impressive. The last person in our circle to share her word was my daughter, Heather. I expected her word to be one that was studious or perhaps flamboyant (she's always been rather dramatic). But she surprised me with a word that I consider rather ordinary. Her word was "pregnant."

I'm not always the quickest person to perceive hints or grasp hidden meanings. I remember thinking, *That's an odd word to bring to our word party. It's not new or different or curious.* THEN I realized what she meant. "I'm going to be a Mimi!"

I was absolutely elated!

Several of my friends had recently become grandparents, and their joy seemed to know no bounds. I had been looking forward to the moment when I would be able to share in grandparenting joy. My turn had finally come! After a full ten minutes of raucous celebration, we all settled into the joy of knowing that many exciting days are yet ahead of us.

Not long after the heralding of such wonderful news, we were informed that our first grandbaby would be a girl. I'm relishing the thought that my first granddaughter is coming soon. Preparations have begun, and the anticipation of the birth of our little one is certainly mounting week by week.

☙ ❧

The anticipation of my granddaughter's birth reminds me of another greatly-anticipated birth. The prophetic arrival of the long-awaited Messiah, the savior of the world, was heralded throughout human history, beginning with the fall of mankind in the Garden of Eden. How beautiful that God would proclaim the solution to our greatest need at the moment of humanity's greatest failure!

In the beginning, in the Garden of Eden, Satan—in the form of a serpent—came to deceive God's children, Adam and Eve. Adam and Eve believed the serpent's lies and rebelled against God. But just as they introduced sin into this world and created separation between God and man, God spoke His solution to redeem man's error.

Because of the serpent's deception, God cursed the serpent to forever grovel in the dust, and then He delivered the promise of the One who would strike the victorious blow against Satan and the effects of sin. That One is Jesus Christ.

> *Then the Lord God said to the serpent, "Because you have done this, you are cursed more than all animals, domestic and wild. You will crawl on your belly, groveling in the dust as long as you live. And I will cause hostility between you and the woman, and between your offspring and her offspring. He will strike your head, and you will strike his heel."* (Genesis 3:14-15)

Jesus would be the One to strike the head of Satan. Although it would be many, many generations (see Luke 3:23-38) before He arrived in human form to offer His life as the final payment for the sin of all mankind, He would surely come.

Although it may have appeared to many that Satan had delivered the final death sentence to Jesus upon His crucifixion, God declared defeat over Satan as He raised His Son from the dead to give us victory over the curse of sin, hell, and the grave. Such victory—such greatness—surely should be heralded in the grandest way. Prophets like Isaiah and Micah foretold His coming, and many who knew the holy Scriptures anticipated His arrival. Luke records in his gospel account that "Everyone was expecting the Messiah to come soon."[50]

God could have announced His Son's arrival with great pomp and circumstance. One might expect trumpeters to go before the Messiah in a great procession as He was revealed to the world. Instead, God chose a different way by selecting a lone man named John to prepare the way for our Savior.

> *Isaiah had spoken of John when he said, "He is a voice shouting in the wilderness, 'Prepare the way for the Lord's coming! Clear the road for him!'"* (Luke 3:4)

50 Luke 3:15a.

John, who was to become known as John the Baptist, was born to Elizabeth and Zechariah, a Jewish priest. Both Elizabeth and Zechariah were very old, and Elizabeth was unable to conceive a child.[51] But an angel of the Lord appeared to Zechariah while he was on duty in the Temple and told him that Elizabeth would conceive and give birth to a son. The angel informed Zechariah that he must name the child John.[52]

At the time of John's birth, Zechariah was filled with the Holy Spirit and gave this prophecy:

> *Praise the Lord, the God of Israel, because he has visited and redeemed his people. He has sent us a mighty Savior from the royal line of his servant David, just as he promised through his holy prophets long ago. Now we will be saved from our enemies and from all who hate us. He has been merciful to our ancestors by remembering his sacred covenant—the covenant he swore with an oath to our ancestor Abraham. We have been rescued from our enemies so we can serve God without fear, in holiness and righteousness for as long as we live. And you, my little son, will be called the prophet of the Most High, because you will prepare the way for the Lord. You will tell his people how to find salvation through forgiveness of their sins. Because of God's tender mercy, the morning light from heaven is about to break upon us, to give light to those who sit in darkness and in the shadow of death, and to guide us to the path of peace.* (Luke 1:68-79)

John grew up and made his home in the wilderness until the time came for him to begin his public ministry.[53] The Scriptures tell us that John wore camel-hair clothes and ate locusts and wild honey.[54] He

51 Luke 1:5-7.

52 Luke 1:8-13.

53 Luke 1:80.

54 Mark 1:6.

preached on the banks of the Jordan River, calling all who heard him to repent of their sins and be baptized.

Great crowds of people came to listen to John preach.

> *All of Judea, including all the people of Jerusalem, went out to see and hear John.* (Mark 1:5)

John's preaching was direct and uncompromising, which made him rather unpopular with the pompous religious leaders. John was calling for a change of heart—true repentance. The Lord had come, and John's message and baptism were preparing His way.

As the people gathered at the river and listened to John's preaching, they desired to know if John himself was the Messiah. But John made it clear he was not—that the One they were anticipating was yet to be revealed.

> *John answered their questions by saying, "I baptize you with water; but someone is coming soon who is greater than I am—so much greater that I'm not even worthy to be his slave and untie the straps of his sandals. He will baptize you with the Holy Spirit and with fire."*
>
> (Luke 3:16)

God's life-mission for John the Baptist was to prepare the way for the life, death, and resurrection of His Son, Jesus Christ. John was willingly different than most people in his appearance, his words, and his purpose. He wasn't caught up in personal achievement, and after Christ was revealed, he knew it was time to allow the people's focus on his personal ministry to decrease as Jesus' ministry began to increase. John told his followers that Christ "must become greater and greater, and I must become less and less" (John 3:30).

Such a life of dedication and sacrifice is unusual when compared to the selfish tendencies of most people. John knew his life-purpose, and that assisted him in staying focused on Christ.

I think the struggle that we often face to live above selfish behavior is certainly due, in part, to our lack of purpose-driven focus. We tend to become focused on the day-to-day concerns of living, and we can easily lose sight of—or never even realize—our life's purpose to point others toward Christ. As Christ's followers, we simply prepare the way for others to know Him.

And that is precisely what John the Baptist did; he prepared the way for the Messiah's arrival into the world. Observing that beautifully executed purpose in Scripture—a purpose performed with such humility—is enough to cause us to call John the Baptist a trophy of God's grace. But I would say that the end of John's life brought even more honor to this title.

John was imprisoned before his death, and it was during his imprisonment that we hear the faint cry of his desperate hope to know that his life had not been wasted. It seems evident that John—like many of us would if we were sitting in that prison cell—had a moment of doubt about his purpose in life.

John had to have understood that the religious leaders and many who followed them had been anticipating the arrival of the Messiah as a conquering hero who would rise up and rescue them from their present Roman oppression. But that is not what John spoke of when he pointed his own followers to Jesus as the One who was coming after him.

However, John was living in a society that was confused about the person of the Messiah. He had to deal with that confusion, and his imprisonment clearly challenged him and his expectations of the future. He knew he was hated by powerful people. He knew his life could be taken from him for his stand for righteousness. He yearned to know that his efforts to do God's will had not been in vain. The contradiction in the minds of many concerning the Messiah as king and the Messiah as a humble man going about preaching and ministering to those in need had to have been difficult to understand. It seems John was trying to make sense of that contradiction as he sat in prison.

> *John the Baptist, who was in prison, heard about all the things the Messiah was doing. So he sent his disciples to*

> *ask Jesus, "Are you the Messiah we've been expecting, or should we keep looking for someone else?"*
> (Matthew 11:2-3)

John's disciples traveled to where Jesus was ministering to ask Him that simple yet profound question. When Jesus received it, He didn't berate John for asking. Instead, Jesus' grace-filled reply was beautifully comforting and surely gave John the assurance he needed to believe he had accomplished the mission God had assigned to his life.

> *Jesus told them, "Go back to John and tell him what you have heard and seen—the blind see, the lame walk, those with leprosy are cured, the deaf hear, the dead are raised to life, and the Good News is being preached to the poor." And he added, "God blesses those who do not fall away because of me."*[55] (Matthew 11:4-6)

Shortly after Jesus delivered those words of reassurance, John the Baptist was beheaded—martyred for the life he lived as the appointed forerunner of Christ. John the Baptist lived his life and ministered to others in a way that pointed people to Jesus Christ.

And so should we.

☙ ❧

Our lives should create a path for others to follow to Jesus. The privilege of pointing others to Christ isn't always easy. It's a life of dedicated purpose and sacrificial living. We, like John, need God's grace to live in such a way that enables others to follow us to the cross of Christ. And as God uses us to prepare the way there for others, we too—like John—become trophies of God's grace.

Today, I wait with great anticipation for the arrival of my precious little granddaughter. She is coming, and the day she is born will be a day

55 "Or *who are not offended by me*"—footnote from the NLT.

of great joy for us. But I await with even greater anticipation the second coming of Christ.

What joy will be ours when we finally stand in the presence of our Savior!

With that anticipation, we join John—that wonderful, faithful, bold trophy of God's grace—in preparing the way of the Lord. We continue to point others to Jesus and proclaim, "Look! The Lamb of God who takes away the sin of the world!"[56]

56 John 1:29b.

CHAPTER 11

Grace to Let Go

THE JOY OF family is a beautiful gift from God. I'm grateful for my children—who are now all adults—and my first grandchild (who, at the time of writing this chapter, has now come into my life).

For about twenty-two years of my adult life, my primary objective was to raise my children well. I think it's safe to say that the goal of most parents is to train their children into mature, productive adults. With that accomplished, the day those children leave home can be both celebratory, as a job well-done, and sorrowful, as an end to the tight-knit family unit with all its members living together.

I remember when our oldest child, Kirsten, left home to attend college in Springfield, Missouri. That's a long, eight-hour drive from Nashville, Tennessee. Anticipating that the dynamics of our family would change significantly when she left, I cried from time to time, thinking about her leaving for nearly a year prior to moving her into her college dorm room.

Kirsten is a people person who draws others to her kind heart like a magnet. The rest of my family—my husband, my daughter Heather, my son Jonathon, and I—are naturally driven, task-oriented people who have had to put great effort toward growing in empathy and learning to intentionally put people above tasks. We learned those things largely from watching Kirsten.

So to say that our family dynamics changed the day she left for college is an understatement. As a mother, I worried not only about how Kirsten would adjust to her new surroundings but also about how Heather and Jonathon would adjust to her being gone. Like most concerns, my worries were much larger in my head than in real life, and I'm glad to say things worked out fine as we continued walking through the days and weeks after Kirsten's exit.

I think my year of crying was also partially due to the fact that Kirsten and Heather are fourteen months apart in age, so I was lamenting that Heather would also be leaving home soon. I knew the family unit as we had known it for so long would continue to change, and it would never be the same again.

I'm grateful I had eighteen years of parenting experience prior to the moments when Kirsten and Heather left home. I had plenty of time to adjust to the idea of letting go.

❧ ❧

Recently, I was reading in the Old Testament about Hannah and how she brought her son to serve in the Temple at a very young age. She didn't have eighteen years to prepare for his departure. And yet she navigated the process of letting go with such grace.

The record of Hannah's story in the Old Testament begins during her childless years of marriage to her husband, Elkanah. Elkanah had two wives, Hannah and Peninnah. Peninnah had borne children, but Hannah was barren. The author of 1 Samuel describes Hannah's painfully difficult situation this way:

> *Each year Elkanah would travel to Shiloh to worship and sacrifice to the Lord of Heaven's Armies at the Tabernacle. The priests of the Lord at that time were the two*

> *sons of Eli—Hophni and Phinehas. On the days Elkanah presented his sacrifice, he would give portions of the meat to Peninnah and each of her children. And though he loved Hannah, he would give her only one choice portion because the Lord had given her no children. So Peninnah would taunt Hannah and make fun of her because the Lord had kept her from having children. Year after year it was the same—Peninnah would taunt Hannah as they went to the Tabernacle. Each time, Hannah would be reduced to tears and would not even eat.*
>
> (1 Samuel 1:3-7)

As I read this, Hannah's plight evokes a sense of compassion in me. None of us want to be taunted, but to be taunted and told that the Lord himself is afflicting us adds insult to injury. Hannah had more than childlessness to deal with. She also had to deal with an accuser whose hurtful words inevitably implied that God was not pleased with her.

Upon first reading this story, I wanted to shout how unfair the Lord was for withholding children from Hannah. But taking the whole story into consideration gave me a different perspective. Instead of seeing God's actions through the critical eyes of Peninnah, I began seeing Hannah and her experiences through the eyes of God's grace.

In retrospect—after reading the rest of the story—we can see that God desired to give His people a great prophet. And when He sought for an honorable woman to give birth to the child who would become that prophet, He found Hannah, who became a willing, spiritual vessel. God was to soon end Peninnah's taunts, and Hannah would have a son.

For her son to become what God wanted him to be, God's plan was for him to grow into adulthood in the Tabernacle under the tutelage of the high priest. Hannah, by necessity, would need the courage and grace to let go of her child at an early age. God knew Hannah was the one He could trust, and she was chosen.

The process through which Hannah yielded to God's plan was painful yet productive. Peninnah's taunting drove Hannah to cry out to God for help.

> *Once after a sacrificial meal at Shiloh, Hannah got up and went to pray. Eli the priest was sitting at his customary place beside the entrance of the Tabernacle. Hannah was in deep anguish, crying bitterly as she prayed to the Lord. And she made this vow: "O Lord of Heaven's Armies, if you will look upon my sorrow and answer my prayer and give me a son, then I will give him back to you. He will be yours for his entire lifetime, and as a sign that he has been dedicated to the Lord, his hair will never be cut."*
>
> *As she was praying to the Lord, Eli watched her. Seeing her lips moving but hearing no sound, he thought she had been drinking. "Must you come here drunk?" he demanded. "Throw away your wine!"*
>
> *"Oh no, sir!" she replied. "I haven't been drinking wine or anything stronger. But I am very discouraged, and I was pouring out my heart to the Lord. Don't think I am a wicked woman! For I have been praying out of great anguish and sorrow."*
>
> *"In that case," Eli said, "go in peace! May the God of Israel grant the request you have asked of him."*
>
> *"Oh, thank you, sir!" she exclaimed. Then she went back and began to eat again, and she was no longer sad.*
>
> (1 Samuel 1:9-18)

God, in His sovereignty, knew that Hannah's pain would cause her to humbly come before Him and make her request. Her desire for a child was so great that she willingly offered to return him in service to God. God used Hannah's pain to prepare her for dedicating her son to His service.

God will also use our pain to bring us humbly before Him. We often don't understand why events and circumstances in our lives don't work out the way we thought they would. But in our confusion and desperation, if we will find our way to humility before our loving Father, He'll direct our situation to align it with His purposes.

Hannah received Eli's words of blessing over her situation and genuinely believed that God would grant her request. Her countenance reflected her heartfelt trust in Eli's reassuring words.

In due time, Hannah gave birth to a son and named him Samuel.

Hannah kept her promise to return her son to the Lord. After Samuel was weaned, Hannah willingly took him to the Tabernacle and left him in Eli's care.[57] She made a promise that she dutifully kept.

Experience tells us that many people make promises to God in their cries of desperation, but many, if not most of them, fail to keep their promises after God delivers them from stressful circumstances. Knowing this makes Hannah's response to God so beautiful.

Hannah's faith and dedication to keep her promise—to let go—is evidence of the generous gift of God's grace in her life. And this can be true for us as well. God's grace—grace to trust that He is good and desires what's best for us—enables us to open our hand and let go of what is so precious to us.

Hannah asked God for a son, promised to give him back to God in service to Him, and followed through on her word. Then, Hannah continued her pilgrimage each year to the Tabernacle and brought Samuel a new coat and the comfort of a mother's love. Samuel grew up in the Tabernacle and became the last judge to Israel before the historical period of the kings.

God honored Hannah for her obedience. He blessed Hannah, and her womb yielded more children as the years went by.

> *Each year his mother made a small coat for him and brought it to him when she came with her husband for*

57 The Scripture tells us Samuel was presented to Eli for God's service after he was weaned (1 Samuel 1:22-24). Children in those days often nursed longer than is usual today in Western societies, and considering that children in some parts of the world still today wean children beyond the age of four, it is possible that, when Hannah took Samuel to the Temple to learn to serve God, he was a toddler between three and five years old.

> *the sacrifice. Before they returned home, Eli would bless Elkanah and his wife and say, "May the Lord give you other children to take the place of this one she gave to the Lord." And the Lord blessed Hannah, and she conceived and gave birth to three sons and two daughters. Meanwhile, Samuel grew up in the presence of the Lord.*
>
> (1 Samuel 2:19-21)

It seems that much of life is about giving back to God the beautiful gifts He's given to us—like the gift of family. Hannah's ability to view the gift of a son from the grace-filled perspective of heaven's purposes is worthy of our admiration. As a trophy of God's grace, Hannah certainly stands as an example of how to faithfully honor God with our most treasured possessions by letting go of them when it is time to do so.

☙ ❧

God's beautiful grace is evident through the stories of people's lives lived to honor God. Like their stories, like my stories, and like yours, the touch of God's presence affects us in so many ways. And as it does, we become trophies of His grace.

EPILOGUE

TROPHIES ARE POWERFUL symbols of victory, and in the hands of our Lord, we become the most beautiful trophies of all—human lives transformed by the grace of God. From the beginning of our lives to the end, we are completely dependent on God's grace. Through His grace, He draws us, saves us, fills us, transforms us, and leads us home.

Throughout the chapters of this book, we have journeyed through beautiful biblical examples of God's grace revealed in the lives of others. We have seen how God delivered Nebuchadnezzar from pride. And we discovered through his story that we can either succumb to man's fallen nature and be consumed with pride in what we've accomplished, or rise above it, choose God's ways, and learn humility.

Jesus Christ gave us the greatest example of humility—love poured out on us through His willingness to die a cruel death on our behalf. I'm so grateful for God's redeeming love demonstrated to us through His Son. Redeeming love pushes past our pride to allow God to reveal Himself more fully to us. That is truly His grace at work!

We have also seen how death stands powerless before our Lord as He raised Lazarus from death to life. Just as Jesus called Lazarus from the grave, so will He call us out of our most painful moments into new life. Grace—the gift of undeserved kindness—is granted to us by the One who has complete authority over death itself. Jesus declared himself true Life. We will one day pass from this earth into eternal life with Christ. But even today—and every day—He provides us the grace we need in our painful and seemingly hopeless situations.

We discovered that, when the Lord tells us to have faith during challenging experiences, like Jairus, we can trust the value of His admonition. God has proven himself faithful over and over again, and we draw on the trust developed over time through our relationship with Him.

God's faithfulness holds us steady as we walk through painful trials in life. We have learned, like Job, that we must maintain our trust in God and our reliance on His character, even in our most difficult moments. We all feel the struggle as we grapple with the difficulties of life and cling to faith in the middle of our pain. But God has proven time and time again that He is more than enough to carry us through every circumstance.

God certainly proved himself to be more than enough in the life of the demon-possessed man who was touched by Jesus and became perfectly sane. We're reminded by that man's story that God actively seeks out and extends grace to those who have troubled minds and needy hearts.

God's intervening grace in our lives is always on time! The woman whose only son had died would certainly agree. When Jesus encountered that funeral procession, He raised the young man back to life as an act of His compassionate grace. How beautiful that Jesus would be so moved by the distress of His creation that He would feel and act with such compassion. And how beautiful it is that every restorative touch of God in our lives speaks of His compassion toward us.

The apostle Paul experienced that restorative touch in the form of right thinking. He was rescued from a misguided thought pattern and set free by Jesus through a corrected perspective. Like Paul, we can easily fall prey to misguided thought patterns, which lead to wrong actions. We, too, need to be rescued and set free.

Transformation in our actions begins with changing the way we think. And our standard of right-thinking is the Word of God. As we allow His Word to transform our thinking, adjust our perspectives, and influence our actions, we are rescued and set free to think and live according to His Word and His ways. His grace has rescued us, and His Word continues to transform our minds.

As we allow His Word to transform our thinking, we learn to depend on God through every circumstance—even through the upsetting of our own plans. Through Daniel's life, we learned that adverse events which force adjustments to our plans are actually opportunities to experience the grace of God in our lives. Our willingness to humbly trust God through those adverse events and changing circumstances positions us to receive something good out of what we consider bad.

John the Baptist had to do that, as well—he had to humbly trust God through confusing and difficult circumstances. We discovered how John lived his life to prepare the way for Christ. As followers of Christ, we too simply prepare the way for others to know Him. We, like John, need God's grace to live in such a way that enables others to follow us to the cross of Christ.

Lastly, we learned from the life of Hannah that God's grace—grace to trust that He is good and desires what is best for us—enables us to open our hand and let go of what is so precious to us. I saw this same grace on display last Tuesday night under the Jefferson Street Bridge.

My dad often goes with me to the Bridge these days. I'm not sure if it's his way of watching over his daughter, in a protective sense, or if he goes simply because he enjoys serving people. Perhaps his motivation stems from a little of both.

As we pulled into the parking lot last Tuesday night, my dad pointed out a bumper sticker on the car that parked in the space in front of us. I knew who owned the vehicle because of the sticker, which displays a girl's name written in a beautiful, cursive script.

My dad's curiosity prompted an explanation from me. The name on the sticker belonged to a couple's young-adult daughter who had died in a car accident about a year earlier. I watched the mother grieve her daughter's death, never blaming God or faltering in her faithfulness in serving others.

My dad was very quiet as I told him about that beautiful family who had experienced God's grace in their situation. As my dad was listening to me, I know he was identifying with their loss because of

God's ever-present help and grace in his own time of need. My dad's grief over my mom's passing has been great, but with God's grace, he is moving forward.

But that wasn't the end of God's grace on display that evening. I took my usual place at the drink cooler where I serve cold juice to our guests. Standing to my right, my dad enthusiastically handed out napkins and utensils. Volunteering on my left that night was a woman we had met previously only once, but that happened to be our night to find out a little more about her.

As we talked and asked questions about each other's lives, she mentioned that she had lost her five-year-old little girl to cancer many years ago. She didn't hesitate to tell us the heart-wrenching story. But she was also quick to speak of God's faithfulness through the whole experience. When a parent buries a child, it is a reminder to all of us that the difficulties of this life can seem unbearable at times. But seeing the peace and joy on the face of such a parent also reminds us that we serve a God whose grace is more than enough in our time of need.

We read in the Bible so much about how God has poured out His grace on mankind as He has cared for, called, and appealed to His creation. But that's merely a taste, a historical introduction, to His marvelous grace and love.

All around us, we observe continuing evidence of God's beautiful grace on display. And in our own lives, we can point to His intervening grace with confidence.

We truly are trophies of His grace.

CPSIA information can be obtained
at www.ICGtesting.com
Printed in the USA
JSHW031403040421
13211JS00002B/8

9 781950 718719